THE DORM ROOM GUIDE

THE COMPLETE HANDBOOK FOR PREPARING, PACKING, AND LIVING WELL IN COLLEGE

THE DORM ROOM GUIDE

LARA BECKER

TEN SPEED PRESS
California | New York

CONTENTS

INTRODUCTION

Hi. I'm Lara, founder of The Dorm Guide.

Even though it has been decades since I was a college student, today I eat, sleep, and breathe dorm and college life.

It all started when my first child went to college in 2021. I had no idea what we needed to do to get him ready to move into the dorm (nor did he), and we needed a little guidance. His small college didn't have much information on its website about dorm rooms or move-in procedures. I managed to find one video of a dorm room that wasn't even in his building, and there was no parent or student Facebook group for the school, either. We were on our own.

The lack of helpful and trustworthy information out there was shocking. Every Google search and Facebook group kept turning up recommendations and suggestions that felt like clickbait—"The 10 Best Mattress Toppers," "The 20 Dorm Must-Haves"—and spammy links to low-quality products.

Thankfully, I love research and planning, so I turned dorm

shopping into a mother-son project. Not surprisingly, my son was far more focused on playing baseball in college than on shopping for dorm room essentials, so I dug in myself and brought him in for the decision-making. I found that I absolutely loved exploring options and preparing him for dorm life and move-in day. It allowed me to reminisce about my own college days, yes, but it also helped me feel connected with my son while we worked on plotting out his dorm room and deciding what he needed together.

We did a pretty good job shopping but a terrible job packing, and we loaded the car all wrong, so we had a somewhat disastrous move-in day. But we worked with his roommate and his roommate's family, and we all did our best to set the boys up for a good year. And wow did I learn a lot from that one day at that one small college as I left my firstborn there. On the drive home, I was hoping we'd taught him everything he needed to know to be out on his own and make good decisions, but that worry would slowly subside. And then I started thinking about what came next.

Clearly there was a great need for a dorm room shopping, packing, and organizing expert. Someone had to take control, turn down all the dorm noise, and provide honest, trustworthy information, recommendations, and how-tos. I decided it would be me.

This is my purpose now. I even built a dorm room in my house, complete with two twin XL adjustable-height dorm beds and all the other "dorm essentials" that I've tested, built, stacked, broken, and squeezed into small spaces over the years.

This purpose doesn't just stem from my experiences with my two kids (yes, two years later I packed, organized, and moved my second son to college, too). I also have the distinct honor of running the Dorm Shopping Recommendations & Deal Alerts Facebook group, which I founded in early summer 2022. I have learned so much of what I'm sharing in this book from the amazing parents and students in the group. There are so many unique experiences, unusual dorm rules, roommate issues, and homesick students after drop-off. Just when I think I've seen it all, the parents and students challenge me with totally new scenarios and questions while they are dorm room planning.

And I am proud to answer every question that is posted. That's my job, and that's how I stay in touch and on top of the dorm trends, the school rules, and which products are holding up and which are not. By late summer, we get to see the amazing move-in photos from families who are so thankful to have found our little corner of Facebook. There are no silly questions, but there are definitely *repeat* questions. The same thirty or so questions are asked over and over, every year. I still smile when I see them—I remember when I wondered those things, too. And I make sure to patiently answer them or direct the poster to where they can find the answer.

The good news is that I've taken all those questions, the best of the answers, the collective wisdom, the trials and errors, the creative solutions, the flat-out mistakes, and the advice about managing the emotional ride that is getting ready for college and turned it into this book.

You don't have to read this book from front to back, although I'd love for you to have all the principles in mind before you match with your roommate, receive your housing assignment, and start dorm shopping.

If you're going to visit the school and can get a dorm tour, don't miss the list of what to ask, photograph, and measure on pages 16–17.

If you're taking a plane ride to college, chapter 3 offers the best advice from years of watching families navigate this like pros.

We'll go through budgeting, where and when to shop, and each important part of the dorm room, including what to know and how to plan, along with creative solutions for small spaces.

Packing and move-in come next, along with important considerations for taking a car to college.

We'll finish up with common post-move-in challenges with recommended solutions and finally how to plan for move-out and next year.

A NOTE FOR PARENTS

Sending your child off to college is an exciting, overwhelming, and emotional experience. You're not alone in this journey though, and this book will guide you every step of the way.

You'll find practical information, tested recommendations, how-tos, and important tips for saving money, reducing stress, and setting your student up for success. I'll also explain how to keep track of researching, budgeting, shopping, and move-in planning.

But let's start with a look at the dorm rooms of today.

Times Have Changed

I remember my freshman dorm room well; I wish I had a photo! My roommate and I didn't get the dorm that we wanted. We got the old building that hadn't been renovated. There was a drab, smallish metal-framed window and two metal beds with well-used damask-covered innerspring mattresses.

As in many dorms, the bathroom was at the end of the hall and shared by dozens of students. That part is a blur, but I'm fairly certain some avocado-colored tile was involved.

My roommate and I bought reversible comforters at Linens 'n Things—kelly green on one side, deep purple on the other. I believe we bought the matching purple sheets, too, which was a definite splurge! We had a small cube fridge and a microwave, along with too many clothes, too much makeup, and probably enough Aqua Net to get us through to winter break, but that was it. My belongings fit in the trunk of my mom's Buick sedan, and move-in day was quick and easy.

My mom dropped me off, helped me load my things onto a luggage trolley, gave me a big hug, and I took it from there. She never even saw my dorm room in person. Fast-forward a few decades, and things are very different.

The dorm rooms of decades past were all pretty much the same: two basic beds with flimsy mattresses, two desks, a closet or two, and a large communal bathroom at the end of the hall. But today there are many configurations, ranging from small singles with private baths to lavish eco-friendly suites with kitchens. The mattresses are still not great, but the good news is that they are bedbug-resistant and easy to clean. Don't get me wrong; there are also still many old-school dorm rooms. I lived in one built in the 1960s, and both of my children's first-year dorms were in buildings built much earlier than mine.

The bottom line is not to make any assumptions until you have your dorm assignment. This book will walk you through what to know about today's dorms, what you must research before shopping, and all those differences, new rules, and tested solutions.

This Is a Time for Learning and Growth

Going to college provides a great opportunity for our kids to learn about researching, budgeting, planning, negotiation, independence, decision-making, adulting, and especially the importance of checking and responding to email!

Handling "no" and disappointment come with college planning, too. *No, you're not allowed to bring that. No, that is way too expensive for a dorm room. No, there isn't room in that class this semester. No, we've given out all the bids for this fraternity or all the spots in the marching band.* The parental protection and blow softening of the high school years isn't there, but this is part of why college leads to growth.

It's hard for us to sit back and watch the struggles and even the big wins from afar, but this is our time to be the cheer squad, not the coaching staff. The sooner students learn to handle things independently, the more successful they will be throughout college.

So get out the pom-poms. You can do it.

A NOTE FOR STUDENTS

Hear me out: "Soiling the nest" is a term used to describe students who, in the two to six months leading up to college, become irritable, snippy, and generally unpleasant at home.

At the very time that your parents are struggling with the thought of you not being home every day, you might be making life kinda miserable for them. Why? Because this is a very common subconscious defense mechanism. You may not even realize it, but you're probably worried about leaving home. The more difficult you make it to live in the same house together—again, subconsciously—the easier it might feel to leave.

Please keep this in mind. You will feel nervous and uncertain about leaving for college no matter what; try to avoid also distancing yourself from your family. Talk to friends, other relatives, a counselor, or a high school teacher, and try to be gracious at home during this emotional and chaotic time.

Keep It Real

This book isn't about creating a Pinterest-perfect dorm room—it's about real students, real families, and practical solutions that work and will last.

If you're planning to go all out for your dorm room, I'm here to support you. But keep in mind that beneath the design, decor, and flair, you'll still need a plan for the practical, functional items, and this book will be your guide to the foundation of your room.

LET'S GET STARTED!

I'll say this over and over, but it's important to remember that each school is different. The guidelines throughout this book take into consideration every situation I've encountered. Still, there will be anomalies out there: schools that do things, allow things, and provide things very different from what is presented here. This book starts with research for a reason: You need to dive deep early on, know your guardrails, and build from there.

As I end every one of my emails to our community, we've got this!

Welcome to *The Dorm Room Guide*!

xo,
Lara

1

Research Is Essential

What You'll Take Away

- → The importance of research in the process of planning for a dorm room
- → A checklist of questions you'll need to ask, and how to find the answers
- → Questions to ask during dorm tours, Accepted Students Day, or orientation

The first step for every student (and parent of a student) moving into a dorm room must be research. Because every dorm is different, every school has different rules, and each student has different needs, I promise that investing in research will pay off down the road. Decisions based on assumptions often lead to headaches and wasted money. This chapter outlines exactly what to research and confirm *before* shopping to create a plan that is specific, compliant, and cost-effective.

Pro Tip: Move-in day is not the time to learn that your bed height isn't adjustable or that your surge protector must be UL Listed (a safety certification; see page 161).

WHEN TO START RESEARCHING

If you've committed to a school, now is a good time to get started. The earlier, the better! Without a dorm assignment, you won't be able to gather many of the specifics. Still, you can find rules and policies relevant to all dorms on campus, and you'll start learning where to find information to make it easier when you get your room assignment. Be sure to log all your research so it's easy to find. In the next chapter, you'll create your own dorm packing checklist (see page 19).

HOW TO ORGANIZE YOUR RESEARCH

Decide where to keep track of the answers to your questions before you start shopping. I highly recommend a cloud-based spreadsheet, so you can access it anytime from anywhere. Set it up, make it shareable, and start to document your findings. I call this master spreadsheet the Dorm Room Organizer. Over the course of this book, I'll explain how to create multiple tabs on this spreadsheet (see pages 19, 20, and 21). But let's start with the first tab on your blank Dorm Room Organizer spreadsheet, the sheet to record your research.

Cloud-based spreadsheets, such as Google Sheets, make collaborating with your family and roommate(s) simple. It is also easy to access when you are out and about and see something you want to buy for dorm life but need to check measurements or rules.

WHAT TO RESEARCH

It can be daunting to scroll through your school's housing pages and all the popular dorm shopping options and come away with any sort of clarity about what is needed for college. This section contains several categories with questions and details for each. You don't have to find answers to all the questions, but the information you gather will help provide direction when it comes to what you need, what will work in your space, and what is permitted.

Dorm Room Layout and Facilities

First things first! You will need to find out the basics: room type, layout, and the facilities available in the room, on the hall, and in the building. You should be able to find most of this information on your school's website from a combination of written descriptions, photos, and downloadable PDFs.

Room Type

If you do not have your specific room assignment yet, can you narrow down the style of the room? (E.g., are you attending a school where all freshmen are in traditional double rooms?) You will likely be in one of the following room configurations: single, double, triple, quad, or suite-style or apartment-style.

Room Size and Layout

While not critical, it is helpful to have an idea of: room dimensions, window location(s), door location, and any fixed furniture or sink areas.

IMPORTANT NOTE: Keep in mind that the dimensions provided on the college website may not be totally accurate, as some rooms may vary. Floor plans are usually not posted for security reasons, but you may be able to find them through nonschool sources.

Bathroom

- Is there a private or semi-private bath attached to your room, or is there a communal bath located at the end of the hall?
- If there is a private bathroom, are the students responsible for cleaning it?
- Does the shower require a shower curtain? What size?
- Is there storage space or a cabinet under the sink?

Closet

- What type of closet space is in the room? You may have: an open area (with or without a rod), a built-in or freestanding wardrobe, or a closet with a door.
- Is there long-hanging space for dresses, long skirts, or pants?

Lighting

- What kind of lighting is in the room? (Dorm rooms typically just have one overhead light.)
- Is there a light in the closet space?
- Is there a provided desk hutch with a built-in light?

Laundry

- Where are the laundry facilities? There could be: a laundry room on each floor, laundry in the basement or on another floor, laundry in another building, or even a washer and dryer in the unit in a suite-style dorm room.
- Is there a cost for laundry? How is it paid? Many students use their student ID to pay (no more coin-op machines).
- What type of laundry detergent is permitted? Some schools allow only liquid detergent or specifically prohibit pods or sheets.

Shared Kitchen

- Is there a kitchen area on each floor, or is there a kitchen somewhere in the building?
- What are the rules for those spaces, and which appliances are allowed in them?
- If you have a suite-style dorm room, you may have a small kitchen or kitchenette in your unit.

Heating, Cooling, and Humidity

- Does the building have air-conditioning?
- Can you control the temperature in your room? Note that while you may see a thermostat in a photo of a room, it may not be operational, or it may not actually control the room's temperature.
- How is the in-room humidity? Almost all dorm rooms are damp, but it is a good idea to find out what students in your dorm building have experienced in prior years.

Elevator

- Almost all dorm buildings are multistory. Is there an elevator in the building, or will you be taking the stairs exclusively?

Furniture Details and Specifications

Most dorm rooms will include a standard furniture package, including a bed, dresser, desk, and desk chair. Some will also have a wardrobe unit (usually when there are no closets). To properly outfit your room, you'll want to find the details of each item, as well as those of any other standard items provided by the school.

Bed Size

- **What size is the bed?** While twin XL is the most common, there are also regular twin, full, and full XL beds in dorms. The larger sizes are primarily found in suite-style dorms with private bedrooms.
- **What is your mattress thickness (in inches)?** Some schools include this in their furniture specs. This information will be helpful in chapter 7, which dives deep into how to layer a dorm bed (see page 92).

Bed Frames and Heights

- What are the bed height options?
  - > Typically, the bed's height is adjustable. Options include:
    - semi-lofted (aka captain's height or raised height)
    - fully lofted (check whether the school will loft the beds or if you have to contract with their approved third-party installer)

        - bunk beds (if you are assigned to a triple or a quad room, bunk beds will likely be involved)
    - For beds that are not adjustable:
        - Are bed risers permitted? If so, how tall?
- What style of bed frame is provided? You may have a boxy wood frame or a more modern metal frame. If the legs are round, you'll want to know in advance.

Dresser

- Is a dresser provided?
- Is the dresser under-the-raised-bed height or taller? Some schools provide two two-drawer stackable dressers that won't fit stacked under a raised bed.
- Is the dresser built-in or freestanding?
- Is the dresser part of a wardrobe unit?
- Are measurements provided?
- Can roommates' dressers be stacked if desired?

Desk

- Are there measurements for the desk?
- Is a desk hutch provided?
- Does the desk have drawers?
- What is the chair like? (If it's solid wood, you may want to pick up a seat or back cushion.)

Wardrobe

If the room has a wardrobe unit:

- Are the dimensions posted?
- Are there photos of the interior?

- Are there fixed shelves or cubbies?
- Is there space for long garments along with short ones, or only one or the other?
- Is anything inside adjustable?
- Are there built-in drawers inside or at the bottom of the unit?
- Is the wardrobe unit itself movable or built-in?
- What is the clearance between the top of the wardrobe and the ceiling?

Pro Tip: Accessibility and Medical Accommodations: For disability-related or medical accommodations, submit an accommodations request through your school's Disability Services as early as possible. Approvals may impact room assignment, furniture provided, and move-in planning.

Is Anything Else Provided?

- Are trash cans and/or recycling bins provided, and if so, what are their sizes?
- Are any appliances, such as a mini fridge or microwave, provided?
- Is there a filtered water option in the dorm? If so, where is it located?

Pro Tip: I always recommend a kitchen-size trash can—a little office-size trash can is just not that useful.

What Are You Allowed to Bring?

When it comes to what you can bring to your dorm room, there are no standard guidelines; the rules vary widely between schools. There is also no standard on where to find these rules or if they will all be in one place on your school's website. You'll need to use extra diligence to find these answers before planning and shopping.

Wall Decor

- What can be used to hang decor on the walls? Some schools allow: adhesive strips and hooks, mounting and poster putty, pushpins (on Sheetrock walls), painter's tape only (for tricks to use in painter's tape situations, see page 226)
- Are there any permanent bulletin boards or bulletin board rails available for hanging decorations?
- Is removable wallpaper permitted?

Window Coverings

- What are the dimensions of the window(s)?
- Are blinds provided?
- Are curtains allowed? If so, are there any requirements for them, such as fire resistance?
- Is the window recessed a bit to allow for a tension curtain rod inside the opening, or would a curtain rod need to go over or around the window?

Appliances

- Which appliances are allowed and which are prohibited?
- Are there appliances that are allowed only if rented through the school? This may be the case for mini fridges and/or microwaves, which are often offered as a single MicroFridge unit.

- If mini fridges are allowed, is there a maximum size in cubic feet (e.g., 3.2, 3.5, 4.0) and/or a wattage maximum?
- If microwaves are allowed, is there a maximum wattage or size in cubic feet (typically either 700 watts/.7 cubic feet or 900 watts/.9 cubic feet)?
- Are any small cooking appliances allowed? Some dorms permit small appliances, such as a coffee maker or an electric kettle, but none with exposed heating elements.

Lighting

- Are LED light strips allowed?
- Are non-LED string lights allowed?
- Are neon signs allowed?

Rugs

- Are rugs allowed? If so, are there any requirements for them, such as fire resistance?
- What sizes work best in this dorm building?

> **Pro Tip:** I recommend only low-pile rugs for dorm rooms. Shag rugs are cute, but they trap dirt, hair, and crumbs and are hard to vacuum.

Personal Furniture Items

If space allows, are furniture items permitted? These could include: nightstands, headboards, chairs, futons (for under fully lofted beds), dressers, mini-kitchen stands, or shelving.

Are there any specific limitations, such as no fabric drawers or a requirement that additional furniture items be under a certain size or weight? Are upholstered headboards or headboards with charging ports allowed?

Electrical Items

- How many outlets are in the room?
- Are there requirements for surge protectors or other electrical items? Many schools do not allow extension cords (only long-corded surge protectors and often with further requirements).
- Are electronics required to be UL Listed?

Safety Tip: Mini fridges and microwaves should always be plugged directly into a wall outlet or surge protector, never into an extension cord.

Door Decor

- Are there dry-erase boards or bulletin boards outside the door in the hallway?
- Are doormats or other door decor permitted?

Items That Are Almost Always Prohibited in Dorm Rooms

- Paint
- Permanent wallpaper
- Candles, candle warmers, incense burners—anything with a flame
- Space heaters

- Portable air conditioners
- Extension cords
- Wi-Fi extenders
- Weapons, alcohol, drugs, smoking paraphernalia, fireworks
- Pets (although service animals may be okay)
- Decor hung directly on windows visible from the outside

Pro Tip: If you have a service animal, contact the housing department at the school to inquire about options. If you are able to bring your service animal to a dorm room that you will be sharing, please be up front about the situation with potential roommates.

THE RULES ARE NOT JUST GUIDELINES

I sometimes hear comments like "Even though air fryers aren't allowed, my daughter loves hers, so we're going to send it with her anyway. She'll just be quiet about using it."

Bringing prohibited items such as an air fryer, candles, or alcohol into a dorm room, thinking they can be hidden, is not a good idea. Those items are prohibited for safety, building code, or insurance purposes. Resident assistants (RAs) do checks after move-in and randomly throughout the year.

The consequences for not following these rules are real, too. If a prohibited item is found, it will be removed and discarded, not shipped back home or held until move-out. If alcohol is found, there will almost certainly be a reported conduct violation with further consequences.

If you love air-fried meals and snacks, hopefully there will be a shared kitchen in your dorm building where you are permitted to make them!

WHERE TO FIND THE ANSWERS

Always start with your school's housing page. It may be referred to as Housing, Residential Life, or something similar. You may have to click through every page and download PDFs to find all the policies, and you likely won't find all the answers on the school's website alone. To complete your list, you may also need to consult the following resources.

> **Pro Tip:** Dorm rooms may vary on the same hall and in the same building. Rules and policies may be revised. Please consider everything you find directional rather than exact!

Parent Facebook Groups

Look for Facebook groups specific to the school. For larger schools, there are probably multiple groups, including one for your specific graduating year. The graduating year group will be helpful for enrollment, registration, and new student questions. For information from those with dorm experience, consider joining a general parents' group for the school.

You can do searches or ask questions such as:

- Are there specific dorms designated for freshmen?
- Can you bring [the item you are curious about]? (E.g., mini fridge, rug, curtains, coffee maker, futon.)
- What are the dimensions of the windows in [the name of your dorm]? Can you fit a tension rod inside?
- What size rugs do people use in this specific dorm?
- Do the dressers move and fit under the beds?
- Does anyone have a picture of the desk chairs provided?

> **Pro Tip:** While it's not a specific school Facebook group, I think you'll love TheDormGuide.com's "Dorm Shopping Recommendations" Facebook group, where I answer questions every single day!

Instagram Accounts

Students should follow:

- The school's Instagram account
- The school Instagram class of (their college graduation year) account
- The school's Instagram housing account

Parents should follow:

- The school's Instagram account
- The school's Instagram housing account

YouTube

YouTube can be a great resource for gaining a better understanding of the dorm rooms at your school. Students from previous years may have posted an unofficial dorm tour to showcase their dorm rooms or simply to help future students.

The university may have videos intended to help future students with planning, especially if the school wasn't able to provide dorm tours during prospective student tours.

Pinterest

In the same way that former students may have displayed their post-move-in videos on YouTube, they may have posted photos on Pinterest.

Search for your college name + dorm, or if you know your dorm building, search college name + dorm building name and see what you find!

Related School Departments

If you are truly desperate for an answer, you can try sending an email to Housing, the RA department, or even Facilities/Maintenance.

DORM TOURS AND INTEL GATHERING

If you have an upcoming visit to a school for a campus tour, Accepted Students Day, or orientation, check whether dorm tours are available while you are in town.

You know the old saying "Measure twice, cut once." If you're lucky enough to get a tour or preview of your school's dorm rooms, measure twice *and* take several photos from different angles. In fact, you should take a video of the entire room as well as photos.

You will likely not be able to tour your exact room or even your building, but bring a tape measure and the list below because even though rooms vary, furniture, mattresses, and window sizes are often the same, or close.

- Room dimensions
- Number of outlets and where they are located
- Exact window dimensions (also note if a tension curtain rod could be used)
- Distance from floor to bottom of window
- Exact height from the bottom of the horizontal bed rail to the floor, especially if the bed is at your preferred height
- Mattress thickness
- The distance between beds that are parallel to each other (helpful for rug sizing and nightstand planning)
- Desktop dimensions
- Desk drawer dimensions and number of drawers. Is there a pencil drawer or a keyboard tray? Take note of whether there is a lock on any of the drawers.
- The space from the bottom of the desk hutch, if provided, to the desktop to determine if a computer monitor or makeup mirror will fit below the hutch. Also measure any hutch shelves or cubbies for bins or other items.
- Sizes, locations, and measurements of any built-in bulletin boards, bulletin board rails, cabinets, or shelves in the room, for bins or organizers
- Closet rod length and height from the floor
- The opening of an open closet, for a curtain rod/curtains to close it off

- The storage areas within a wardrobe (think baskets, bins, hanging organizers). The depth of the unit. Take note of whether there is a lock on the wardrobe.
- The available storage space below the sink (minus the pipes), if there is one in the room. If the area under the sink is open, measure the height from the bottom of the sink to the floor.

Key Actions to Take

- ☐ **Schedule a dorm tour if you'll be visiting campus.**
- ☐ **Scour the housing pages and linked documents.**
- ☐ **Determine if housing or enrollment deposit timing impacts your timing to select a dorm room.**
- ☐ **Join and follow important social media accounts and groups.**
- ☐ **Create your research log. This is the first step toward creating your dorm packing checklist even if you don't have your dorm assignment yet.**

2

How to Create a Dorm Packing Checklist

What You'll Take Away

- **The recommended spreadsheet layout to create your own packing checklist**
- **The ten things every student will need for college, to get you started**

Every year, parents and students are bombarded with "ultimate" lists of must-have dorm essentials from ads, blogs, retailers, influencers, and Pinterest pins. Some may even try to sell you a dorm checklist. But these lists are generic, often commission-driven, and not tailored to your dorm setup, rules, or personal preferences. They are optimized for clicks or ad revenue, not for you.

In chapter 1, you did your homework. You asked a lot of questions and learned about your room's details and rules. This chapter turns those facts into a personalized checklist for dorm room planning and shopping that feels like it was designed for you—because it was!

HOW TO BUILD YOUR CUSTOM DORM PACKING CHECKLIST

In the previous chapter, you did the research on your dorm room. Now it's time to set up your just-for-you dorm room plan and shopping list. Even if your dorm assignment is months away, you can still get started.

Build a Spreadsheet Using This Template

You've likely already created the cloud-based spreadsheet (see page 2): your overall Dorm Room Organizer.

It will eventually have multiple tabs. The first tab will be for research, and the next for your dorm packing checklist. This is where you'll begin today, creating columns for each of these considerations. And as a reminder, you can find a spreadsheet template on TheDormGuide.com:

- **Category:** Use categories such as Bedding, Studying, Bathroom, Kitchen, Electronics, Storage (Clothes/Shoes, Jewelry, Makeup, Haircare, Locking Storage), Laundry, Cleaning, Air Temps and Quality, Decor, Safety, Car.
- **Item:** Name of the item (Twin XL Mattress Topper, Desk Hutch, Storage Drawers, Laundry Hamper).
- **Need:** Consider three priority levels to help with budget planning: "Must-Have," "Nice to Have," and "Wait and See," with the latter for items that you can wait until after move-in to see if they're necessary. Be sure those are not in the list of items that sell out early every year (see page 57).

- **Dimensions:** Add details about the sizes you need or the sizes you've purchased.
- **Space:** Use "Fits" and "Check" on the sheet to ensure that the item will work with the measurements found during research.
- **Rules:** Use "Okay," "Unsure," or "No" to guarantee that you've checked any specific requirements found during research, such as maximum size, electronics certifications, and what is/is not allowed.
- **Source:** Use "Purchase," "Borrow," or "Bring from Home."
- **Budget:** Add in your allocated budget for this item.
- **Price:** Include the actual price paid for the item.
- **Shared Item:** If this is something that will be shared with a roommate or roommates, indicate that with a Y/N in this column. (See page 77 for a list of items typically shared by roommates.)
- **Status:** Use "Need," "Purchased," or "Packed." You will want that Packed status to keep track of what's made it into a bag headed to college.
- **Purchase Information:** Indicate where each item was purchased, the purchase date, the shipped-to location if ordered online, and the return date. Trust me, once the boxes start arriving, you'll want to keep track of what you've already purchased, and the dates will help you coordinate any return windows.

HOW TO CREATE A DORM PACKING CHECKLIST

	A	B	C	D	E	F	G	H	I	J	K	L
	DORM ROOM ORGANIZER: DORM PACKING CHECKLIST											
1	CATEGORY	ITEM	NEED	DIMENSIONS	SPACE	RULES	SOURCE	BUDGET	PRICE	SHARED ITEM	STATUS	PURCHASE INFORMATION
2	Use categories such as Bedding, Study, Bathroom, Kitchen, Electronics, Storage (Clothes/ Shoes, Jewelry, Makeup, Haircare, Locking Storage), Laundry, Cleaning, Air Temps & Quality, Decor, Safety, Car.	Name of the item (Twin XL Mattress Topper, Desk Hutch, Storage Drawers, Laundry Hamper).	Consider three priority levels to help with budget planning–"Must Have," "Nice To Have," "Wait and See," with the latter for items that can wait until after move-in to see if they're necessary. Be sure those are not in the list of items that sell out early every year (page 57).	Add details about the sizes you need or the sizes you've purchased.	Use "Fits" and "Check" on the sheet to ensure the item will work with the measurements found during research.	Use "OK," "Unsure," or "No" to guarantee you've checked any specific requirements found during research, such as maximum size, electronics certifications, and what is/ is not allowed.	Use "Purchase," "Borrow," or "Bring from Home."	Enter your allocated budget for this item.	Enter the actual price paid for the purchase.	If this is an item that will be shared with roommate(s), indicate that with a Y/N in this column. See page 77 for a list of items typically shared by roommates.	Use "Need," "Purchased," "Received," or "Packed." You will want that Packed status to keep track of what's made it into a bag headed to college.	Once purchased, indicate where it was purchased from, the purchase date, the shipped-to location, and the return date. Trust me, once the boxes start arriving, you'll want to keep track of what you've already purchased, and the dates will help you coordinate any return windows.

THE NEED/SPACE/RULES APPROACH

It's important to remember that dorm shopping involves considering and purchasing many items—a lot of little things, a few bigger purchases, and an occasional splurge. There will be planned purchases, impulse buys, and scouring for the hard-to-find items. I promise you that at some point, you'll lose track of what you've ordered and what you still need. You may forget some of the early research you did and inadvertently purchase something that turns out to be against the rules.

Three columns in your dorm packing checklist are the "Need," "Space," and "Rules" columns. To help you evaluate items, build your checklist, and keep track of purchases. As you build your list, these three questions will help guide what makes the list and what does not: Do you need it? Do you have space for it? And is it allowed?

BEFORE YOU BUILD YOUR LIST: ADDITIONAL CONSIDERATIONS

Before you start to put items on your list, there are a few more things to think about, which were not specifically explored in your research phase (see page 3).

Personal Preferences

Beyond the dorm setup itself, each student has unique needs and preferences that no generic dorm checklist can anticipate. I recommend considering current habits. (Hoping that new habits will start when college does is probably not realistic.) Here are some personal needs and preferences to consider.

- **Personal Habits:** Take into account sleep preferences such as mattress firmness, temperature, sounds, and darkness, as well as hygiene and personal grooming practices and dietary requirements and routines.
- **Study Style:** Some students need a full desk setup, while others prefer studying in the library and setting up their desk as a hair and makeup station.
- **Extracurriculars:** An art student will have different storage requirements and room setup priorities from a golfer. Animal science majors and workout enthusiasts may need to consider hazmat-level laundry hampers.
- **Medical Needs:** Students may need locking storage for prescription medications or a room free from feathers and scented items. Until you know your roommate assignment, it is best to wait before buying anything that could trigger allergies or asthma.
- **Seasonal Wardrobe Requirements:** Is the school in a cold-weather climate near skiing, or a warm and sunny beach school? Distance from home to school factors in here as well for seasonal wardrobe changes.
- **Food and Cooking Preferences:** Even with an unlimited meal plan, you'll need to have storage for some amount of food and drink in the dorm room. Coffee drinkers, late-night studiers, and athletes need varied setups, too.

Those college dorm checklists floating around the internet don't account for any of these room or personal variables! The lists may come with good intentions, but no two students will have the same list. Buying blindly from what appears to be a colorful and organized checklist will likely lead to wasted money and move-in day headaches.

Let's shift the mindset from "What do people typically bring?" to "What do my room and my routine require?"

How Long Will You Live on Campus?

The number of years you'll spend in on-campus housing determines where to invest and where to spend sparingly for a freshman dorm room.

I always recommend planning for as much reuse as possible from dorm room to off-campus living as you build your dorm room checklist. The first step toward this goal is to know the general plan for all four years.

Some students are required to live on-campus for all four years, while others may spend only one year in on-campus housing due to limited availability.

Others may spend time in Greek housing, or studying abroad, or in longer co-op or intern engagements.

Why does it matter? The length of time you'll spend in a dorm room with a similar setup will factor into your choices about how to allocate your budget.

Save or Invest?

If dorm life is one year and done, here are some things you might want to save your money on, and other things that might make sense to invest in.

INVEST IN: Closet storage, room storage, bathroom storage, towels, an air purifier, a fan, small appliances, electronics, lighting, health and safety items, desk accessories, hair/makeup/jewelry storage, locking storage.

SAVE ON: Bedding, a headboard, a nightstand (if there's a raised bed height), wall decor, a laundry hamper, a rug, curtains.

NOTE: Bed sizes may change even if living on campus for multiple years.

- These recommendations assume a twin XL mattress for dorm life and a larger size for off-campus living. If siblings are heading to college in the near term, some of the items may be repurposed. Decor and rugs will probably not be reusable.
- If you'll be living on campus for multiple years, are there suite-style (apartment-style) dorm rooms for upperclassmen? Do the bed sizes change? Do the suite-style dorm rooms have kitchens?
- If the bed size and room type will remain the same for multiple years, add a mattress topper and dorm room kitchen setup to your list of investments.

Will You Have a Single Dorm Room?

There are three types of single dorm rooms:

1. A Dorm Room Built as a Single
   > With a scaled-down size and a single set of furniture for a single student, these rooms are often quite small, but they're all yours. It is important to understand the room dimensions and furniture layout before starting your list.
2. A Double Dorm Room Meant for Two Students but Assigned to One Student as a Single
   > This style of room may be assigned to students with accommodations or other situations requiring a single assignment.

> Check with the school to determine if both sets of furniture will remain, and if so, if you are allowed to use both sets. Some schools require that the second set of furniture stay in the room but not be used. If the second set of furniture is available to use, students will often push the beds together, as two twin XL beds exactly equal the dimensions of a king bed.
> If you can use both sets of furniture, that will significantly impact your list, as you'll have far more storage with two dressers, two desks, and potentially a king-size bed with plenty of storage space below.

3. A Single Bedroom in a Suite-Style Dorm Room
   > These often include private or semi-private bathrooms, and sometimes come with a common area and even a small kitchen space.
   > In addition to outfitting your dorm room (bedroom, in this case), you'll also need to bring the essentials to set up your bathroom and, if applicable, the common area and kitchen. Hopefully, if you have roommates, you'll connect with them early in the process and can work together to divide up the list of necessities to bring.

Will You Be in a Suite-Style or Apartment-Style Dorm Room?

If you're heading to a suite-style or apartment-style dorm room, congratulations! I know you will enjoy the benefits of potentially a private bedroom, a living area, an in-suite kitchen, and a private/semi-private bathroom. (Oh, by the way, you'll have to clean that bathroom . . . see chapter 16 for everything you need to know about cleaning.)

The following is a list of additional considerations for a suite-style dorm room.

- **Bedroom Setup (Single or Double):** Is furniture provided? What type of closet space do you have? Do the bedroom doors have individual locks or keypads?
- **Bathroom Configuration:** Does each bedroom have its own bathroom, or is there a semi-private bathroom shared by multiple bedrooms?
- **Bathroom Layout:** Is there a shower/tub combo or a shower stall? How many sinks are there, and is there storage below the sink(s), or space in the room for additional storage?
- **Common Areas:** Is there a shared living area with provided furniture? What size couch or chairs are provided? (I recommend bringing stretch furniture covers.) Is there room for a TV console table and TV?
- **Kitchen Space:** Which appliances are provided? What other appliances are permitted? (The prohibited list should be much shorter for suite-style dorms than for traditional dorms.) Is there a dining table or breakfast bar? How much cabinet storage is available? Is there a pantry?
- **Cleaning:** Confirm that private or semi-private bathrooms will not be cleaned by school personnel and that this is the responsibility of the students. Then stock up on cleaning supplies, a decent vacuum cleaner, and a mop!

START ADDING ITEMS TO YOUR DORM PACKING CHECKLIST

Okay, now is the time to start adding items to your spreadsheet. Begin with items that you may have already determined you want during the research phase, due to student interest, or because they are an obvious necessity, such as bedding and towels.

Then work through this book, chapter by chapter, and record items of interest in this spreadsheet.

Run each item that you add through the Need/Space/Rules test. Do you *need* this item? Will it actually work and fit in the space, and does it comply with all the dorm rules?

For specific product recommendations, feel free to visit my website, TheDormGuide.com, to browse the full Dorm Essentials Guide.

Pro Tip: Never split the cost of dorm items with your roommate(s). If one person buys a majority of the items and collects a share of the cost from the roommate(s), dividing the items at the end of the year becomes very tricky. Instead, split up the list into roughly equal total costs. At the end of the school year, everyone is responsible for the items they brought.

What to Do If the List Is Getting Out of Hand

Both students and parents can get a bit carried away when planning for a dorm room. I know, it's fun! If the list is becoming excessive, review the below discussion points and look for potential compromises.

- Remember that dorm rooms are small, trends are short-lived, and the student will live in this room for only about nine months, excluding several breaks.
- Consider the care and cleaning of items in the dorm room. I strongly advise against shag/fluffy rugs, dry-clean-only comforters, and appliances requiring regular, detailed cleaning.

- Walk through each category and think about the student's current habits, personal needs, preferences, and expectations for college life. College is expensive; it's okay to rough it a bit during dorm life! Reconsider the must-have status for nice-to-have or wait-and-see items.
- Think about reusability. Will the student be living in a dorm room for multiple years, or is it likely they will head off-campus after one year? Prioritize options that will work in future living situations.

THE TEN THINGS ALMOST EVERY STUDENT NEEDS (AND SHOULD BE PERMITTED!)

If you're anxious to get started with your list or even do some early shopping for an eighteenth birthday or high school graduation, the following are the ten items that almost every student will need, will use, and should be allowed to bring.

1. **Sturdy Moving Bags:** I prefer those with backpack straps for ease of carrying.
2. **Fan:** Almost all dorm rooms are stuffy and warm.
3. **Quick-Dry Towels:** Dorm rooms are damp, too, so quick-dry towels are the best.
4. **Air Purifier:** Dorm rooms are often damp and germy, and sometimes moldy. Choose an air purifier that is appropriate for 150 to 200 square feet from a reputable brand to last through college and beyond.
5. **Tool Set:** Not just for move-in day; it really does come in handy.
6. **High-Powered Portable Charging Block:** College students' devices get a workout every day.
7. **Personal Safety Devices:** Key-chain alarms, pepper spray, drink covers. Check your campus policy to be sure all are permitted.

8. **Easy-to-Clean Water Bottles:** Water will likely come from filtered water dispensers around campus, so stainless steel water bottles are helpful. Be sure to choose wide-mouthed versions, preferably without hard-to-clean straws or complicated tops.
9. **Luggage Set:** A nice luggage set is a thoughtful gift at any time, especially for those attending college far from home.
10. **Weekender Bag:** For quick trips to visit friends, a school activity, or a weekend visit home.

Key Actions to Take

- ☐ **Add the Dorm Packing Checklist to your cloud-based Dorm Room Organizer spreadsheet.**
- ☐ **Review sophomore through senior year housing options for your school or schools of interest to determine how many years you may be living on campus.**
- ☐ **Take note of special considerations for single dorm rooms.**
- ☐ **Share the spreadsheet between the student and family (and maybe even future roommates) to help with dorm planning.**

3

Long-Distance Planning

What If You're Flying to College?

What You'll Take Away

- → The travel and logistics to consider ASAP
- → The five shopping options for long-distance moves
- → The four dorm essentials to buy while you're at home over the summer
- → Options for shipping direct to your dorm or college town
- → How to pack dorm essentials for a flight

When college is an airplane flight away from home, everything gets a bit more complex—shopping, move-in, returns, repairs, medical care, breaks, and move-out, too! Without a plan, distance can add stress (and high shipping fees). This chapter gives you an efficient shopping and packing plan. I've seen many nervous long-distance students and families have positive experiences over the years, and you can too!

BEFORE YOU SHOP, RESEARCH TRAVEL AND LOGISTICS

No matter the distance to school, research the timing and process for signing up for orientation and move-in dates as soon as possible. If your student has committed to a school far from home, please consider these factors before beginning dorm planning and shopping.

- Orientation often occurs during the summer before the school year begins. Larger schools will have several weeks to choose from, and there may be a priority order for selecting your week based on factors such as the date of your enrollment deposit or honors college admittance. Compare the available weeks to your schedule and the price of airfare. If you're many months away, set up flight price alerts to let you know of any price drops.
- Is there a specific move-in date or week for freshmen? If the family will be traveling, too, go ahead and book a hotel or Airbnb now, as they will likely be in high demand and expensive. Be sure you can cancel with no charge if plans change. Accommodations with laundry facilities can be helpful if you need to wash new bedding and towels.
- Consider a one-way drive for move-in. Some families choose to make the long drive to school in a rented minivan or SUV, and then the parents fly home after move-in. A family road trip to college can be a memorable (and hopefully fun!) experience. If this is a consideration, book the car ASAP. You can always cancel later, and rental car prices typically increase

gradually as the rental date approaches. If you are a member, Costco Travel often has good car rental deals.

- There is likely a Parents' Weekend at the school four to six weeks after move-in. Check the school calendar and decide if you can attend, or at least book a hotel room that can be canceled later. Go ahead and bookmark that school calendar page on the school website!
- Book rental cars as far in advance as possible if you'll need them for school visits.
- Oh, and while you're looking at the school calendar, confirm the dates for breaks, *including* the dates that dorms close.

Avoid This Mistake

A long-distance student has their last exam on the last day of finals, a Friday. To give them a little breathing room, their parents book their plane ticket home for the following day, Saturday. But as the end of the semester approaches, they find out that the dorms close on that Friday! They end up scrambling to pay a hefty airline change fee or book a hotel for one night. Always check the school calendar!

SHOPPING OPTIONS FOR LONG-DISTANCE STUDENTS

There are a number of different options for when (and where) to buy what you need for your dorm—and you'll likely want to shop with a mixture of them all in mind:

- Buy at home. Bring the items with you, or ship them to college before move-in.

- Buy and ship directly to local friends or family, a roommate, or a package-holding service.
- Buy online closer to move-in with shipping to school or your hotel if they have a package hold program.
- Buy locally after arrival.
- Buy and ship during/after move-in.

Below is my recommended timing for purchasing some of the most popular items for dorm rooms. Items that typically sell out early are indicated with purchase-by dates. The full list of items that sell out early or get more expensive is on page 57. This list is subject to change based on supply and demand.

Item	Buy at Home (If Flying)	Buy at Home (If Shipping or Driving)	Buy Online and Ship to Local Friends or Family	Buy Online and Ship Ahead to School*	Buy Locally After Arrival	Wait for Move-In
Bedding and towels	✓	✓				
Mattress topper (purchase by July 15)	✓	✓	✓			
Nightstand (purchase by June 1)		✓	✓	✓		
Desk hutch (purchase by June 1)		✓	✓	✓		
Over-fridge shelving (purchase by June 1)		✓	✓	✓		
Headboard (purchase by June 1)		✓	✓	✓		

LONG-DISTANCE PLANNING

Item	Buy at Home (If Flying)	Buy at Home (If Shipping or Driving)	Buy Online and Ship to Local Friends or Family	Buy Online and Ship Ahead to School*	Buy Locally After Arrival	Wait for Move-In
Storage drawer towers (purchase by July 1)		✓	✓	✓		
Cube organizers (purchase by July 1)		✓	✓	✓		
Storage ottoman (purchase by July 1)		✓	✓	✓		
Large makeup mirrors		✓	✓	✓		✓
Air purifier		✓	✓	✓		✓
Mini fridge			✓	✓		
Microwave			✓	✓		
Rug			✓	✓		
Decor	✓	✓	✓	✓		✓
Small appliances				✓	✓	✓
Toiletries					✓	
Cleaning supplies					✓	
Vacuum cleaner					✓	✓
Food and drinks					✓	

* If the school offers this service. Please check for the earliest ship date to determine whether to ship online purchases to school or to local friends and family based on the purchase-by dates. If the school does not offer this service, check college Facebook groups to determine if there are local companies that will accept and hold packages for you.

Dorm Essentials to Buy at Home

There are a few dorm essentials that you'll want to buy at home (in-store or online) due to availability, the need to wash items in advance, and lead time for custom decor.

Bedding: After purchasing, take it out of the packaging, feel it, and ensure that your student likes it. Then wash, fold, and place in a moving bag to bring to college. Quality nontoxic twin XL bedding gets harder to find online as we move through the summer, and especially in-store near college campuses at move-in time. Bedding recommendations are on page 92.

Mattress Topper: The popular mattress toppers for college beds gradually increase in price and ultimately become hard to find toward the end of the summer. I recommend purchasing one early, removing it from the shipping box (but not the wrapping!), and packing it securely in the thick plastic packaging for transportation to college.

Towels: I recommend quick-dry towels because dorm rooms are typically damp and don't have great places to hang towels to dry. One drawback to quick-dry towels is that they tend to shed more, especially in their first couple of washes. Run them through the laundry separately a few times before packing them for college. Towel recommendations are on page 192.

Decor: If you are ordering custom decor, you may need to place your order early due to uncertain production and shipping schedules. You'll also want to check the items for accuracy and quality.

How to Pack: Flying Your Dorm Items and Personal Belongings to College

Moving bags are the greatest invention for college moves, regardless of whether you are driving, shipping, or flying. The bags hold up to fifty pounds, weigh almost nothing, are easy to carry, and can be folded down and stored easily in the dorm room after move-in. They also pack nicely in the car as they are not as rigid as a box or a plastic tote.

You will need six to eight bags for a typical move by car. Consider a ten-pack if you'll be flying, as you'll want to place any heavy bags in a second bag.

Will you be visiting for a Parents' Weekend in the fall, with the opportunity to bring items like winter bedding, clothes, and shoes later? Bring home a couple of the moving bags after move-in (fold them up to fit in your carry-on), and use them to bring back a full bag of winter gear on your next visit. Maybe there will be a little room left for some of your student's favorite homemade treats, too.

Using Moving Bags as Checked Luggage

Moving bags can be checked in with the airlines—they are too big to take on the plane as carry-ons. I love the moving bags with backpack straps as they are easier to carry and allow you to move multiple bags at once: one as a backpack, and one over each arm.

Prior to travel, double-check the airline's rules for checked luggage allowances and sizes, especially if you'll be flying internationally.

Assuming each family member takes two checked bags, a carry-on bag, and a personal item, I suggest the following: The student's carry-on bag can be a rolling suitcase that can also be used for trips back and forth between college and home. Their personal item can be their backpack, and they can check two moving bags. Family members should pack for the trip in their own carry-on suitcases, and then each check two moving bags.

Fill the moving bags with bedding, towels, clothes, shoes, small personal items, a fan, foldable bins, hair and makeup needs, and school supplies.

For reference, you should be able to fit a comforter, a blanket, two sets of sheets, a mattress pad, and towels in one moving bag. You can vacuum-pack the linens and clothes to save even more space when packing.

Place heavier bags zipper-side down in a second bag. You can also add a boot tray or a folded piece of cardboard from a shipping box in the bottom of the bag to provide a bit more stability for heavier bags or bags with loose items.

Consider using a small TSA lock to keep the zippers closed, and brightly or uniquely colored handle wraps or luggage straps so you can easily recognize your bags on a busy airport baggage carousel. Be sure to label the bags clearly on the outside with your name and phone number. Baggage carousels near large colleges will be filled with moving bags during move-in time!

Shipping Dorm and Personal Items from Home to College

If you need or prefer to ship items from home to school, I recommend packing them in moving bags and then placing the bags in boxes for shipping. The bags are much easier to move and carry once you've arrived, and you'll use them repeatedly throughout college.

Look into the following two shipping alternatives to find the right one for you.

1. College Boxes: This division of U-Haul will ship and hold your boxes to be delivered on your agreed-upon date. This is often a more affordable option than others.
2. Pirate Ship: This (free) online service helps you price out options using the major shipping carriers. You print the label at home and drop off the boxes at your post office or UPS store. The downside here is that you'll need someone on the other end to receive the boxes. You may be able to ship just before you leave and time it to arrive at your dorm, hotel, or Airbnb once you are there.

Twin XL mattress toppers will become harder to find and likely more expensive as the summer progresses. Memory foam mattress toppers are vacuum-sealed in thick plastic and then placed in a box. You can remove the topper from the box for transportation, but be sure to keep it sealed in the original plastic so that it doesn't expand.

Buy Online and Ship Direct Options

Determining your ship-ahead options now will help you determine your shopping timeframe. When the big sales start rolling around in the spring, you're going to want to jump on those deals. If you have a plan in place, you can.

To get a jump on early shopping deals and beat the sell-outs, you have three options:

1. **Ship ahead to school.** A few schools will accept deliveries as early as June 1 for fall semester students. Check the timelines, policies, and any associated costs.
2. **Ship ahead to a local company.** This is an emerging service near larger schools. Local service companies will accept and hold

your shipments during the summer for a fee and then deliver the items to your dorm or apartment at the date and time of your choosing. Some of these companies also offer pack-and-hold services over the summer. It will be pricier, but if you can ship online orders directly to them and avoid paying to ship or fly with the items later, it might be more cost-effective. Check the parent Facebook groups for the school for local company recommendations.

3. **Ship ahead to local friends, family, or roommates.** If you have a friend, family member, or roommate who lives within an hour or two of the school, perhaps they will graciously allow you to ship to their home and hold items for you until move-in time. You'll need a rental car (or minivan) to pick them up upon arrival for move-in, and be sure to bring the person who held them a small token of appreciation. They've saved you a lot of money in shipping or storage fees!

For buying online within a week or two of move-in, there are a few options.

1. **Check with your hotel.** Some hotels near colleges will hold items you ship to them in advance.
2. **Check with the local big-box stores.** If they have some inventory remaining, they may be willing to hold your pickup order longer than stated online.
3. **Check back with the school.** If they didn't have ship and hold options in the early summer, perhaps they do offer them within a week or two of move-in.

Shop for Dorm Essentials Locally After Arrival

"We'll just go dorm shopping when we arrive in town for move-in."

I've personally been in several big-box stores near big and small schools during move-in week, and they are often picked over, busy, and messy. If you can avoid shopping for popular dorm items the week of move-in near campus, please do!

Bedding (especially twin XL), storage drawers and bins, closet organizers, adhesive hooks, rugs, mini fridges, microwaves, fans, air purifiers, and school supplies will be slim pickings at best, or completely sold out at worst. Also, keep in mind that there is a smaller selection in a store than you will find online—for example, even if you can find a microwave, it might not meet the school size limit or wattage requirements. Ordering ahead allows you to properly research your items and ensure that they meet all necessary criteria.

If you must shop locally and you have access to a car, consider driving at least twenty minutes away from campus for a better selection (but still keep expectations in check!). The closest college to where I live is about an hour away, and the college essentials at our local Target are just about wiped out by mid-July. If you want to shop for toiletries, cleaning supplies, snacks, and drinks, shopping locally will be fine. Items that aren't dorm- or college-related should be in decent supply.

Shop After Move-In

Consider waiting to buy items on your list that aren't urgently needed or don't require assembly assistance on move-in day. You might even wait on a few items that aren't immediately necessary (unless they are on the sell-out list).

For those remaining items, you can place an order right from the dorm room. Allow an extra few days and up to a week longer than standard delivery times, as you will not be the only ones with this idea, and the campus mailrooms are completely overwhelmed during those first few weeks of college. Between online shopping orders and packages arriving with items accidentally left at home, give your mailroom some grace!

SUMMER STORAGE AFTER THIS SCHOOL YEAR

It is never too early to think about storage for next summer because units can sell out, or as demand intensifies, rental duration minimums can increase (to far longer than you need). I encourage students to speak with other long-distance (often referred to as OOS—out of state) students and consider sharing a unit with a few of them. Book early!

In recent years, local companies have been emerging near larger schools that offer a service to pick up your items at the end of the school year, store them for you over the summer, and then deliver them to your new residence the following school year. This will likely be more expensive than storing them yourself, but you will not need a car or have to move anything yourself. Be mindful not to leave anything of significant value or that is breakable with the moving companies.

Key Actions to Take

- [ ] Add school dates (orientation, move-in, breaks/dorm closures, family weekends) to your family calendar.
- [ ] Confirm school and third-party ship-ahead policies.
- [ ] Reach out to friends or family near the school to ask if they have the space and are willing to hold shipped items for you.
- [ ] Book important travel ASAP, especially lodging and rental cars that can be modified without penalty later.

4

How to Budget for Your Dorm Room

What You'll Take Away

- Price ranges for the most common dorm essentials
- How to include shared roommate items in your budget
- A proactive plan to reuse, resell, recycle, and donate

A comfortable, functional, and stylish dorm room doesn't require a big price tag. Whether your budget is a few hundred dollars or considerably more, the goal is the same: to invest in quality essentials that you'll actually use. The priorities should be comfort, safety, and functionality, with special consideration for items you can reuse for future years in dorms or off-campus housing.

Most students live in their freshman dorm for about nine months (closer to seven and a half months when you factor in school breaks). Keep this in mind as you prioritize your spending, especially if you expect to live on campus for only one year.

In this chapter, we'll take the following five steps to develop your budget.

1. Level set the funding sources for dorm setup.
2. Research the approximate cost of each item.
3. Revisit your "Need" level for each item.
4. Total your estimated costs.
5. Evaluate, negotiate, and reprioritize as necessary.

WHO IS PAYING FOR THE DORM SETUP?

It's a loaded question, I know. But as you put your budget together, it is helpful to know how much will be funded by the parents, graduation gifts, grandparents, and the student. The earlier you have this discussion, the more time the student will have to work and save for those splurge purchases that don't really meet the must-have criteria.

YOUR DORM PACKING CHECKLIST IS YOUR BUDGETING TOOL

If you haven't already worked through chapter 1 (research) and chapter 2 (creating your custom dorm packing checklist), doing so will be helpful for coming up with your budget.

Use the budget column of the dorm packing checklist to enter estimates for each item. If you have already researched some costs, use those; otherwise, find the list of current year price ranges of the approximately thirty most common dorm essentials listed below on my website, TheDormGuide.com.

This is a good time to revisit your "Need" column. In light of the growing list, discuss what are truly must-haves, what are nice-to-haves, and what can be a wait-and-see. Also, take another look at the dorm rules and ensure that everything on your dorm packing checklist is allowed and meets the required specifications.

Bolded items in the list below of the most common essentials indicate things that roommates often share. Additional information on items to share between roommates is provided on page 77.

Mattress topper
Mattress pad
Sheets (two sets)
Comforter
Pillow
Laundry hamper
Under-bed storage (two units)
Fan
Bath caddy or storage
Towels (two sets)
Surge protectors (two)
Cleaning supplies
Nightstand
Ottoman
Closet storage
Air purifier
Desk/bedside lamp
Jewelry/makeup/hair storage
Mini fridge
Microwave
Kitchen utensils and storage
Simple wall decor
Large trash can
Moving bags
Mini-kitchen shelving
Desk hutch
Rug
Curtains and rod
Small appliances (if permitted)
Vacuum cleaner
More extensive decor

ADDITIONAL ITEMS TO CONSIDER FOR YOUR DORM ROOM

I work with thousands of families each year to help them get ready for college. As you set your budget, I want to make you aware of other common items that students bring to dorms. The list above is a good start of the most common, but many other frequently purchased items are listed below. Please refer to chapter 1 (research) to ensure that you have all the necessary rules and information; this is good input for additional discussion and consideration for *your* list.

Mattress encasement
Blankets
Throw blankets
Throw pillows
Headboard
Bedside caddy/shelf
Bed rail for lofted bed
Comfortable desk chair
Lounge chair
Futon
Utility carts
Drawer carts
Safe for personal items/medication
Shoe shelves
Over-the-door organizer
Drawer organizers
Shower shoes
Bathrobe/bath wrap
Boot tray for wet caddies
Slippers
Shower curtain for private bathrooms
Dehumidifier for known dampness/mold
Desk accessories
Lap desk
Makeup mirror
iPad/AirPods/AirTags/Apple Pencil
TV
Roku stick or Fire Stick
Mobile TV stand
First aid kit/OTC meds
Microwave cooking accessories
Water filter pitcher
Stainless steel water bottles

Clear bag for stadium and arena events
Luggage
Weekender bag
Toiletry bag
Tool set

Beyond the dorm room setup, you'll also want to save for a laptop and backpack if you need new ones for college. Please check the laptop requirements of the department of the student's major before purchasing a laptop for college.

SPLITTING SHARED-ITEM PURCHASES WITH ROOMMATE(S)

Many of the more expensive items in the lists above are items that you will have only one of in the room. Hopefully, you will be in contact with your roommate over the summer to discuss the dorm room and plan shared items.

I recommend creating the list of shared items together with your roommate, then splitting the list so that you each spend roughly equal amounts. Refer to the list of commonly shared items on page 77. Bottom line: Split the list, not the costs.

EVALUATE, NEGOTIATE, AND REPRIORITIZE AS NECESSARY

If you're having trouble bringing the budget into line, take a pass through your list and identify which items you can use for multiple years.

As discussed in previous chapters, find out what the typical housing plans are for sophomores, juniors, and seniors, especially since many schools only have enough on-campus housing for freshmen. Using the lens of reusability may help guide decisions to invest in certain items.

Where to consider investing if you'll be in the dorms for multiple years:

- Mattress topper if bed size remains the same throughout
- Mini-kitchen setup, as dining hall fatigue will progress
- Desk hutch
- Air purifier

Where to consider investing for one year of dorm life and then off-campus housing:

- Air purifier
- TV
- Mini fridge—many students use their dorm fridge in their private bedrooms in off-campus housing
- Small appliances

TRACK ACTUAL SPENDING

Once you start shopping, add the actual cost, purchase date, retailer, and return date to your dorm packing checklist (page 21). This will help you compare where you saved and where you went over budget, keeping your spending on track.

> **Pro Tip:** Add items that need to be returned to your calendar, and set a reminder alert prior to the return-by date.

INSPECT PURCHASES UPON RECEIPT

As items ordered online arrive, open the packages and inspect each item.

- Does it look and feel as expected?
- Are all the parts in the box?
- Is there any visible damage?
- If it is electrical, plug it in and verify that it works properly.

If there are any issues, they will be easier to resolve immediately than if you wait to discover them on dorm move-in day. You'll also still be within your return window, giving you time to make an exchange or a different purchase.

What to do with unboxed items and how to pack them for transportation and move-in is explained on page 247.

Key Actions to Take

- ☐ **If you don't have your dorm packing checklist started, now is the time to create it!**
- ☐ **Start adding estimated costs for each item in the budget column.**
- ☐ **Review and agree on budget and funding sources.**
- ☐ **Add calendar notes to identify return-by dates.**

5

When and Where to Shop

What You'll Take Away

- Shopping tips and suggestions when searching for dorm essentials
- The important nontoxic and safety certifications to look for
- Which items to buy during which months based on years of historical tracking
- The best places (including free ones) to shop for college supplies

Now that you've built your custom dorm packing checklist (page 21), you're ready to shop for your dorm room. But . . . how? Where? I've spent years perfecting how to find the best-quality dorm essentials at the best prices, before the items sell out for the summer. In this chapter, I go over the ideal timeline, the primary retail players (and what to shop for at each), what you can buy early, and how to explore secondhand shopping and resale strategies.

Please keep in mind that this planning guide and information are about reducing stress, not creating more of it. Yes, the best deals come around early, but you may not be ready to buy early if you don't yet have your dorm assignment and a complete shopping list. Don't worry! I promise there will be deals after you finalize your plan. Try to make this an enjoyable experience during this exciting yet emotional time.

Before we go through the timeline and retailer details, allow me to make these three recommendations before you hit "add to cart." It's important to keep the shopping process simple, organized, and safe.

1. Focus on What Matters

It's easy for students to get swept up in comparisons. Social media is full of five-figure designer dorm rooms, and once you've watched a few of these videos, the algorithm will feed you that type of content around the clock. Those setups are unaffordable for most. Instead, prioritize comfort, safety, function, and staying within a reasonable budget.

2. Stay Organized and Shop Wisely

- **Keep your receipts.** Save the online receipts to a College Receipts folder in your mail app.
- **Update your dorm packing checklist.** Note the purchase date, last return date, and retailer in your list. Trust me, you think you'll remember, but it will become a blur!

- **Join free loyalty programs.** You may receive extended return windows, rewards, member-only deals, and presale notifications.
- **Read the reviews before making a purchase.** It sounds simple, but I've spent years reading product descriptions and customer reviews. I skip products with too few reviews, with negative reviews, or with reviews that don't seem genuine.
- **Research the product's seller.** Given that many retailers have adopted marketplace platforms, check the seller, seller reviews, and return policies for each product before purchase.
- **Comparison shop.** Just because you see something on sale at one retailer doesn't mean theirs is the best price. Search the product name and model and see what else you can find. Maybe the item is the same price elsewhere, but there may be a retailer that has more generous return policies or offers reward points.
- **Learn to use Google Lens and Amazon Lens.** Search for products by image using these tools. This is helpful if you see items on other sites that you want to search for elsewhere.
- **Designate a staging area.** The boxes and shopping bags will start piling up, and they will need a dedicated space. For me, it was my dining room each time.
- **Set up a return box or bin at home.** As soon as you decide something won't work, put that item in the return bin so that it doesn't get forgotten about or misplaced.

Pro Tip: Save your smaller shipping boxes to use for care packages during the school year!

3. Prioritize Safety: Look for Important Certifications

With so many products manufactured overseas, often without stringent regulations, look for products with recognized independent safety and materials certifications. The following are the certifications I look for when purchasing items for dorm rooms, college apartments, and my own home.

Product	Certification
Comforters, sheets, mattress pads, blankets, pillows, towels	OEKO-TEX certified
Memory foam products, including mattress toppers, pillows, and dog beds	CertiPUR-US certified
Electronics and appliances	UL or ETL Listed
Nonstick cookware	PFAS, PFOA, PTFE, lead, and cadmium free

TIMELINE: WHEN TO SHOP FOR DORM ESSENTIALS

Some of the most common questions parents ask are “When should I start shopping?” and “What can I start buying early to spread out the spending?” It’s tricky: Shopping too early can be trouble since you really need to know your dorm and the rules, but waiting too long can mean items may be sold out or go up in price due to demand.

Pro Tip: A quick word on shopping near campus during move-in week: Please don’t make this your plan A! By that time, the college aisles of the big-box stores near campuses—and, honestly, in most cities around the country—are well-picked-over, and the stores are packed. It might seem helpful to wait to purchase storage items, mini fridges, towels, and bedding near school, but you will be disappointed with the selection, if any remains.

Based on years of tracking historical market timing and trends for dorm and college essentials, the next section outlines what to expect month by month.

January to March

Start researching (see chapter 1). If you don't have the final school decision yet, familiarize yourself with the top contenders. Look up their dorm selection and assignment process, timeline, and any advantages of putting a housing deposit down earlier than later. Understand the likelihood of, or requirements for, continuing to live on campus beyond freshman year.

For each school, look through potential dorm layouts (and costs) for freshmen, furniture setups, and rules and policies, and have early discussions about what the student truly needs versus wants. Start laying out a budget and expectations. Discuss the importance of reusability beyond year one.

Because this is the "off-season" for dorm shopping, inventory is high and prices tend to be lower for many of my favorite dorm essentials; however, some essentials won't be fully replenished by a few of the retailers until springtime. Note that retailers like Target typically don't fully reset the twin XL sheets, plastic drawer towers, or cube organizers and bins until mid-spring.

By March, some students will have their dorm assignments. And yes, I know we're not even at decision day yet, but those early acceptance and early decision students are moving ahead! Amazon typically has Spring Prime Days, and Target typically has a Target Circle Week sale event in mid to late March. This is a good time to purchase essentials that will work regardless of dorm assignment.

April to May

Many students will have their dorm assignments by the end of May, but some won't have them until a few weeks before move-in or as late as move-in day.

Seasonal dorm items will start to arrive, and roommates will begin connecting and planning together. If you prefer to shop in-store, now is a good time. Big-box stores, even those far from college campuses, will have well-picked-over college aisles by June in many areas.

For those who have their dorm room information and have done their research, now is a great time to shop and take advantage of spring deals before summer dorm demand kicks into high gear.

Memorial Day weekend sales often feature discounts on small appliances, bedding, electronics, and storage solutions.

June

June is a big month for dorm shopping, and the retailers know it. Selection is still mostly stable, especially online, for the majority of dorm essentials. Return windows extend into August or September for some retailers and purchases. If you have your plan and see a good deal, especially on items that tend to sell out or increase in price, don't wait!

Around the end of June, Target has historically offered a one-time 20 percent off entire purchase coupon for verified college students. The coupon is valid on almost anything sold and shipped by Target, but it can sometimes be difficult to get college student verified. You can find hints and tips shared by students who have gotten verified in the past on TheDormGuide.com.

Popular Dorm Items That Typically Sell Out by Early June Each Year:

- Tall nightstands with charging ports
- Desk hutches
- Seasonal dorm merchandise, particularly storage and decor
- The perfect over-fridge wire shelving unit
- The good twin XL mattress toppers
- Full XL bedding
- Upholstered twin headboards with legs
- Select backpack styles

July

Prime Day is the headline. Expect two intense deal days! Many of my favorite items will go on sale, but not necessarily at their lowest price; we tend to see prices at their lowest before July.

Target, Walmart, Best Buy, Kohl's, Wayfair, and others typically run a big-deal-week campaign around the same time, with competitive pricing.

By late July, many of my favorite dorm essentials are either sold out or have limited inventory with higher pricing.

August

August is move-in month for the majority of students. If you've had the benefit of knowing your dorm assignment for months and being able to do preliminary research, you'll be in "fill in the gap" mode by August, and that's a good thing!

Now is a good time to stock up on cleaning supplies, health and wellness items, last-minute decor, and finishing touches. Keep receipts organized, and remember that return windows are still open.

September to October

For students attending schools on a quarter system rather than a semester system, September is probably your move-in month. I also realize that some of those schools don't provide your dorm assignment until you're packing the car to head to college. It is frustrating, but bring the basics, and adjust accordingly after move-in. The good news: We should see some restocks by the time you are ready!

Amazon typically runs a fall deal event in early October. And if history repeats itself, Target, Walmart, and other retailers will follow suit with their own (usually longer) sale events. This is a great time to pick up dorm fixes, care package items, and early holiday gifts.

November to December

It's the holiday shopping season, and the great news is that I've found some of the best deals on college and dorm essentials during early Black Friday, Black Friday, Cyber Monday, and December sales events.

The bad news is that very few of you will be in dorm shopping mode during this time. If you are starting school in January (a spring semester start), you are in luck!

Dorm Items You Can Buy Early

This list includes items most students will use regardless of their room's layout or their housing situation. These items should be permitted in the majority of schools, although there may be a few exceptions.

- Moving bags
- Tool kit
- Doorstops
- Quick-dry towels
- Bathrobe/bath wrap
- Slippers (I recommend only those with indoor/outdoor soles)
- Slim hangers
- Air purifier
- Fan
- Desk lamp—a UL Listed lamp should be allowed at almost any school
- Tabletop dry-erase board
- Jewelry box/storage
- Apple AirTags for iPhone users
- TV—choose a 40- to 50-inch one for dorm room and eventually off-campus use
- Personal safety items such as personal alarms and drink covers
- Coffee maker*
- Electric kettle*

- Water bottles and water filter pitcher
- Vacuum cleaner
- Umbrella
- Luggage
- Toiletry bag
- Weekender bag
- Clear bag for stadium and arena events
- Car safety items—dash cam, portable jump starter/tire inflator

** Check the rules of your schools of interest first; a few don't allow any appliances at all.*

WHERE TO SHOP

Welcome to a Marketplace Economy

Let's start with an explanation of e-commerce marketplaces before we jump into retailers.

Many of today's major online retailers have opened up their online storefronts to third-party sellers. Amazon popularized this model, but now Target, Walmart, Macy's, Kohl's, Best Buy, Home Depot, and others have expanded to allow outside sellers to sell their products on their platforms.

While third-party sellers are vetted to some degree, shipping, warranties, exchanges, and return policies are typically set and handled by the seller. Where Target may offer a free ninety-day return policy, a seller on their platform may offer only thirty days and may charge a fee for returns.

Product photos and descriptions are created by the seller, and in many cases, the seller ships directly to you.

There are some sellers that I've become very comfortable with over the years. I trust them; they produce high-quality products and stand behind them. There are also many that do not.

When shopping online, always look to the right, near the price, for seller information. You should also see return policies and be able to click on the seller's name for more information. If you can keep most of your purchases to items "sold and shipped by [retailer]," you'll eliminate many potential complaints and headaches around quality, items not being as described or taking weeks to arrive (or never arriving), and sellers that won't exchange or return items. For most retailers, you can filter your search by "sold by" or "retailer."

Major Retailers and Their Dorm and College Offerings

Amazon

Amazon is the largest marketplace in the world, with the broadest selection of products for dorms and college. Amazon Prime membership offers very fast shipping, sometimes even same-day delivery, depending on your location and proximity to Amazon's warehouses. You can probably purchase about 80 percent of your dorm packing checklist on Amazon—some of the big things and almost all of the little things. More than 60 percent of Amazon's sales are from independent third-party sellers.

With so many third-party sellers and an open platform, stick with well-reviewed items and brands you recognize for the best quality.

Amazon and its sellers frequently adjust prices to match supply and demand. I've tracked about five hundred dorm items daily for years, which is why I am confident in the list of what sells out early and what increases in price as move-in day nears.

Amazon also offers Lightning Deals, which expire in either twelve hours or when the seller's allocated quantity is sold, whichever comes first. Gift card deals sell out incredibly quickly. Some Lightning Deals are great buys; some are simply a different presentation of the typical price.

Amazon has four major sale events each year (subject to change):

1. End of March
2. Prime Day in mid-July
3. Early October
4. Black Friday/Cyber Monday, which can run for ten to twelve days straight

The other retailers typically wait for Amazon to announce their event dates, and then will announce their own, "coincidentally" during the same week most of the time.

The following are items I don't recommend purchasing on Amazon because they are less expensive or of higher quality at other outlets, which may also offer better return policies.

- Plastic drawer towers and carts
- Wooden cube organizers
- Quick-dry towels
- Some small appliances
- Mini fridges
- Trash cans, especially kitchen-size ones
- Food, snacks, and beverages
- Everyday personal care items
- Laptop computers—buying directly from the manufacturer or your campus bookstore may have warranty and other benefits that are not available from Amazon

Premium Membership for College Students

For years, Amazon has offered Amazon Prime to college students for a free extended trial period, followed by 50 percent off an annual membership. Today, this is known as Prime for Young Adults.

Return Policy

Amazon's standard return window, currently thirty days, is shorter than that of many competitors. The return window is even shorter for certain electronics and other categories, so be sure to check those before making a purchase.

Target

Target is a good option for everyday needs and dorm essentials, especially when they release their inventory each summer. Their dorm aisles and online selections tend to be a bit later than those of other retailers because they are busy with Mother's Day, Memorial Day, and Father's Day, and then they shift to college.

Many of the items that are best to avoid buying on Amazon are better suited for purchasing at Target. In addition, many Target-owned brands' bedding and linens carry OEKO-TEX certification. This verification ensures that the product is free of harmful levels of hazardous substances and is required for it to be on my recommendation list.

Target currently offers special recognition and exclusive offers to college students, educators, and military members. Members of each of these groups must go through an online verification process. Once you have the required college credentials, you should apply. It can take a couple of attempts to be approved.

The college student appreciation program offers year-round

offers "just for college students" and a onetime 20 percent off storewide purchase offer during the summer.

Premium Membership for College Students

Target's premium shopping membership, Target Circle 360, is often available at a discount to verified college students. It is worth checking out for both the two-day and same-day delivery options, as well as an extended return window and other member benefits.

Return Policy

Target has historically offered a very generous 365-day return policy for its own brands, provided a receipt is presented. These include the college-friendly brands Room Essentials, Brightroom, and Threshold. Other items sold and shipped by Target have ninety-day return windows, while marketplace sellers may have shorter return windows. Please carefully verify the return policies for each item.

Walmart

Walmart's strength lies in offering everyday low prices on household staples and groceries. There are fewer dramatic markdowns and big sale events on dorm and college items, but the everyday prices are very reasonable.

My favorite items for dorms at Walmart include storage, laundry, and kitchen items. Walmart's third-party marketplace is significantly larger than Target's, so I encourage you to carefully review the seller, return policy, and product ratings before making a purchase.

Premium Membership for College Students

Walmart's premium shopping membership, Walmart+, is often available at a discount to verified college students. It is worth checking out for both the two-day and same-day delivery options, as well as other member benefits.

Return Policy

Most items sold and shipped by Walmart have a ninety-day return window, while marketplace sellers' return policies may be shorter. Please verify the return dates for each item carefully.

Warehouse Clubs

When you consider small dorm rooms and warehouse-size products, they don't really mix well. However, there are a few exceptions.

Sometimes the clubs surprise me with in-store seasonal products that are a great deal for college dorms. I've seen summers with great deals on mini fridges, folding saucer or butterfly chairs, and water filter pitchers. Then the following summer, none of those things returned.

Warehouse clubs can be a great place to purchase laptops and tablets thanks to their generous return policies and post-sale price adjustments. Before buying a laptop for college, please confirm the required technical specifications from the department of the student's major at their school.

Specialty, Discount, and Regional Retailers

HomeGoods can be a good source for bedding, but confirm that the packaging indicates OEKO-TEX certification. IKEA has a few popular items, and the big-box home improvement stores offer rugs, bedding, and appliances. However, be sure to shop online for the best selection.

You may stumble upon a great collapsible laundry basket, shower caddy, or shelving unit at an Ollie's, Menards, or Aldi. Inventory typically varies by store, but keep an eye out if you're visiting these stores during the summer.

A Note on Dorm Bundles

Bundles. Kits. Packages. You probably know what I'm going to say here. That's right, I'm not a fan. Bundles often trade quality for quantity. Check carefully for materials used, important bedding certifications, and your actual needs and dorm rules before considering a dorm bundle.

Shop Your House First

This is a common phrase I see in our Facebook community, and it makes total sense for some items. Here is a list of what you might find in your house for your dorm room, and keep in mind that when the student moves off-campus, there will be a new level of shopping your house. Start thinking about that new couch or kitchen table set. . . .

- **Comforter and blanket**—you probably don't have twin XL bedding at home, but your dorm bed is likely a twin XL. You can still use a full or queen blanket and comforter, but your sheets and mattress pad should be the exact size of your mattress.
- **Pillow(s)**—in fact, I recommend bringing the pillow(s) from home that you already love!
- **Hangers**—preferably slim profile

- **Trash can**—preferably close to kitchen-size; don't bother with office-size
- **Towels**—preferably quick-drying
- **Desk organizers**
- **Desk lamp**
- **TV**
- **Fan**
- **Vacuum cleaner**—if not too bulky
- **Coffee maker**
- **Rug**—check sizing for the dorm room

Shop on Buy Nothing and Resale Platforms

Don't underestimate the benefits of shopping secondhand. Not everything needs to be brand-new! Ironically, many of the dorm items resold at certain times of year are, in fact, brand-new.

You may already be familiar with Facebook Marketplace in your area. Now is the time to expand your "area," though, if you live near a college campus or not too far from the college you'll be attending.

When to Shop Resales

About a month before the last day of the spring semester, many resales will be posted on Facebook Marketplace groups in the school area. If you are an easy drive from campus, join those groups and start watching for posts six to eight weeks before the end of the school year. Bonus: Even if you don't buy something, you'll see many photos from freshman dorm rooms as the freshmen try to sell the items they won't need the following year.

If you're far from campus but live near another college, you can join those groups, too, and you might be able to find something closer to home. Your usual local Facebook Marketplace groups may have a few items if a student didn't sell items before coming home for the summer, so it is worth keeping an eye on those as well.

What to Buy at Resale

My favorite resale buys are desk hutches and nightstands. The nice desk hutches that match dorm desk sizes are pricey when purchased new and will not be as necessary once you move off campus. The tall nightstands that work great next to raised-height (aka captain's-height or semi-lofted) beds won't be as useful once you move off campus to a typical-height bed. You can pick up desk hutches and nightstands for a bargain in the late spring near a large campus.

You'll also see rugs, bedding, mattress toppers, and decor for sale. I'm okay with the framed wall art resales, but I'm more hesitant about bedding and mattress toppers because those are harder to clean and sanitize. I'm also hesitant about rugs because they typically live a really rough freshman year, and let's face it, they were probably not regularly cleaned or vacuumed.

Please Be Aware of Safety and Scammers

Before you engage with a seller online, please read all current advisories and educate yourself on the latest scams. Never prepay for items when meeting in person, and only use platforms with buyer protection when buying shipped resale items.

If you are purchasing online or through Facebook, always meet in a safe, public, well-lit location, such as a police or fire station, and bring someone with you.

Shopping for dorm life doesn't have to be overwhelming. By following the timeline, mixing big-box and secondhand options, and sticking with safe, reputable products, you'll save money and stress.

And remember, generous return windows give you flexibility, so pay attention to those policies.

Key Actions to Take

- ☐ Confirm when your dorm assignment will be available and consider that against the timeline in this chapter.
- ☐ If you haven't previously bought from a third-party seller on a major retailer's website/app, spend a few minutes familiarizing yourself with how they show up in the product listings.
- ☐ Join free loyalty programs or sign up for emails from retailers you expect to use for dorm shopping.
- ☐ Learn to use Google Lens and Amazon Lens.

6

Roommates

Matching & Planning

What You'll Take Away

- An approach for honest roommate matching
- Tips for living harmoniously with a roommate, whether they're a close friend or a complete stranger
- An understanding of what can be shared by roommates to reduce dorm setup and ongoing supply costs

Roommates shape a surprising amount of first-year college life—from sleep and study rhythms to how peaceful "home" feels after a long day. Sometimes a roommate becomes a lifelong friend, sometimes it's a cordial co-living arrangement, and sometimes, in extreme situations, a change may be the only answer.

I believe the lifelong-friend outcome is rare; there are no expectations that you and your roommate will become best friends. What matters most is creating a workable, comfortable environment where both students can rest, study, and thrive.

In this chapter, I cover how to match well with a roommate and make the best of an assignment and how to plan for shared items so you save money and headaches at the end of the year.

MATCHING AND LIVING WELL WITH YOUR ROOMMATE(S)

There are many different roommate situations in today's college housing options. You may have a single with no roommates or a four-bedroom suite with seven roommates, but likely it will be somewhere in between. While traditional doubles are still the most popular living arrangement, you definitely can't assume this will be yours.

Record first-year class sizes are creating on-campus housing shortages for some schools. The lack of available housing can lead to one of two outcomes—forced triple and quad occupancy in double dorm rooms or some freshmen needing to secure off-campus housing. Neither is ideal, but you can make the best of it. In each of these cases, you may have more than one roommate.

Suite-style or apartment-style dorms are also becoming increasingly popular. These setups can include private or shared bedrooms, private or shared bathrooms, and common areas such as living rooms and small kitchenettes or full kitchens. These are almost always multiple roommate situations.

Roommate Matching Techniques

There are a few schools that do not allow roommate selection and will assign you a roommate, often not revealed until close to move-in day. This is uncommon, though, as most schools allow you to select a roommate or go through a matching process to find a roommate.

Roommate selection and assignments may happen in several ways:

- Room with friends from high school or other existing acquaintances
- Choose a living-learning community or honors dorm
- Match through designated Instagram admitted students accounts
- Participate in survey-based roommate matching through the school

Compatibility Matching: Honesty First

Whether you participate in a formal housing survey, which is kind of like a dating app but for roommates, or an informal process over social media, please be honest with your responses.

- Avoid making statements like "flexible about anything." This may feel polite, but it could backfire down the road.
- Well-written messages and thoughtful replies are stronger signals than perfect photos or high follower counts on social media.
- If special conditions apply, share them clearly and respectfully to indicate that these are not "preferences" but requirements for well-being.
- If you intend to bring a service animal, please be up front about it. I recently learned of a situation in which one room-

mate brought a service cat, while another roommate was allergic to cats. Unfortunately, the school was not quick to remedy this situation.

The following are the types of questions you'll see on a housing survey or should plan to discuss with potential roommates. Being aligned in advance on these questions will help ensure a smoother living arrangement.

1. Sleep Habits
    - Do you like the room dark and quiet at night, or do you sleep with lights or sound?
    - Do you get up when the alarm goes off or are you a multi-snoozer?
2. Lifestyle and Daily Habits
    - What's your daily routine like? Are you an early bird or a night owl?
    - Do you prefer the room to stay quiet, or would you like a little background noise, like music or TV?
    - How clean and organized do you like to keep your space?
    - Are you a phone-and-FaceTime person, or do you prefer to text or Snap with family members and friends?
    - Are there any routines, like prayer or meditation, that you'd like me to know about?
    - Do you drink, smoke, or use other substances?
3. Study Habits
    - Do you prefer studying in the room or somewhere like the library?
    - Do you need complete silence when studying, or can you focus with a little noise and activity?
4. Personal and Social Preferences
    - Do you have any allergies (like to perfumes or certain foods)?

    - What's your stance on borrowing or sharing items?
    - Would you like to host people in the room, or would you prefer it to be just us most of the time?
    - How often do you think you'll go out at night, or do you prefer staying in?
5. Conflict Resolution
    - How do you usually handle conflicts or disagreements?
    - Are you comfortable discussing issues immediately, or would you prefer to address things in a calmer moment later?
6. Boundaries and Expectations
    - How do you feel about having overnight guests (friends, partners, etc.)?
    - Do you think we should have a roommate agreement to lay out boundaries?
7. Fun and Personality
    - What do you like to do for fun? Any favorite shows, music, or hobbies?
    - What's something you're looking forward to in college?
    - How would you describe yourself in three words?

Set Expectations: Workable, Not Perfect

There really are no perfect roommates, especially when you're living together in a room that will be each of your bedrooms, study areas, living rooms, kitchens, closets, and dressing rooms. Add in that dorm rooms are often too warm and probably damp/humid, academic stress is always on the table, and making new friends is hard. Go in knowing that it will not be all sunshine and roses.

A "workable" roommate match is one in which each person can

reliably sleep, study, and feel respected. Communication and setting expectations up front is the best way to get off to a good start.

Complete a Roommate Agreement

It doesn't have to be formal or extensive, but a one-pager with your agreed-upon expectations is a good idea. Hopefully, you'll never have to refer to it, but if you have issues, you'll have the agreement to refer to or bring to your RA.

Your college may have a template to use, or you can find one online.

You'll likely want to include some of the following examples:

- **Sleep and Noise:** Establish quiet hours and lights-out expectations.
- **Guests:** Provide notice for drop-in guests and ask permission for overnight guests.
- **Neatening Up:** Suggest a ten-minute weekly room reset and clean.
- **Sharing:** Beyond appliances, establish boundaries for sharing food, drinks, makeup, jewelry, clothes, shampoo, etc.
- **Health/Safety:** Include allergy prevention, what to do if one of you is not feeling well, use of windows and fans, and keeping the door locked.
- **Expenses:** Think about purchasing trash bags, cleaning supplies, paper towels, toilet paper (if applicable), and shared food, and how that will be equally distributed during the year.

You should each sign the document and take a photo so it's on both of your phones. Plans can evolve, so just update the agreement and photo when they do.

Money and Manners

- If you owe someone money, pay promptly—within twenty-four hours if possible. It is so easy now with the various cash apps. If a friend pays for pizza at 2 a.m., send your portion right away.
- Avoid nickel-and-diming over small consumables. Consider trading tasks (taking out trash, cleaning) to avoid imbalances. Don't let $2 for paper towels get under your skin.
- Say thank you often and truly mean it. Courtesy and gratitude can go a long way toward keeping the peace.

EVERYTHING IS A LEARNING EXPERIENCE

NOTE FOR STUDENTS: Discomfort doesn't mean failure or that you're being unreasonable. Communicate early, be specific, propose a solution, and follow up once. If the pattern continues, escalate appropriately. You'll experience similar situations throughout your career, and this is good practice for conflict resolution.

NOTE FOR PARENTS: Be a sounding board, not a conflict manager. This is my advice for all things college, including roommate issues. Coach your student to speak for themself; this is practice for adult life. If there are issues requiring escalation, that's what RAs are there to facilitate.

PLANNING FOR SHARED ITEMS WITH ROOMMATES

A great way to reduce the cost of dorm room setup is to share the cost of items you need or are allowed to have only one of in your dorm room. You can also share the costs of some of the supplies you'll need during the year. The method you use to share these costs is important. Please be sure to read that section at the end of this chapter.

Please check your school and dorm rules—some of the items may not be allowed or, as with fridges and microwaves, may only be used in your dorm room if rented through the school.

In addition, some schools do not allow outside furniture or rugs or require them to be flame-retardant. Some require electrical items to be UL Listed and plugged into surge protectors only, with a minimum number of joules and a limited cord length and number of outlets. Rules vary greatly, so please double-check yours!

Typical Shared Dorm Room Items

- Mini fridge
- Microwave and microwave-safe cooking accessories
- Mini-kitchen setup—shelves, bins, etc.
- Water filter pitcher
- Coffee maker
- Kitchen-size trash can
- Air purifier
- Dehumidifier or humidifier
- Rug
- Window coverings and curtain rod or tension rod
- Shared seating (e.g., a futon under a lofted bed)
- Full-length mirror (if wanted but not provided)
- TV and TV stand (if wanted)
- Streaming device such as a Roku stick or Fire Stick (if wanted)
- Floor care items (vacuum cleaner, mop, broom, etc.)

Shared Cleaning and Room Staples

You can also save space and avoid duplicate purchases by coordinating the purchasing of cleaning and cooking supplies with your roommate(s). Here are some items to consider sharing:

- Disinfectant wipes and multi-surface cleaner
- Paper towels
- Dish soap and sponges
- Hand soap (if you have an in-room sink or shared bathroom)
- Plates, cups, and silverware
- Food storage containers
- Trash bags

Set up a simple system for restocking shared items to keep your space functional and clean. While you're setting up that system, also discuss a system for emptying the trash can as soon as it is full.

Semi-Private Bathrooms

If you have the luxury of a semi-private bathroom—meaning one that's attached to your room rather than a communal bathroom at the end of the hall—you are likely responsible for setup, supplies, and cleaning. There are a handful of schools that clean the bathrooms *and* provide toilet paper, but these are the exception—count yourself lucky if someone else is cleaning that bathroom!

As you may be sharing the bathroom with suitemates or others beyond your roommate, the acquisition of the items on the below list should be shared by everyone who uses the bathroom. You definitely don't need four shower curtains or toilet brush sets.

- Tension rod for shower curtain (if not provided)
- Shower curtain, shower curtain liner, curtain rings
- Bath mats/rugs—quick-drying and more than one is a really good idea
- Showerhead caddy or other in-bath storage
- Toilet brush set
- Extra hooks for wet towels
- Over-toilet storage shelving
- Small trash can
- Toilet paper
- Cleaning supplies

Suite-Style/Apartment-Style Dorm Common Areas

If your space includes common areas such as a living room or kitchen, you'll need to consider additional items that are likely to be shared among roommates. You certainly don't need all the items on this list, but it should give you good discussion points.

- Extra seating for the living area
- Extra lighting for the living area
- TV and a stand for the living area
- Surge protector(s) for the living area
- Rug for the living area
- Decor for the living area
- Dinnerware and silverware
- Cookware and bakeware
- Cutting boards and knives
- Kitchen utensils and gadgets
- Measuring cups and spoons
- Small appliances

- Starter set of spices
- Food storage containers and supplies
- Pot holders and dish towels
- Cleaning supplies

Methods for Sharing Costs

Start by agreeing on which items will be shared among roommates and suggested specs or features. For example, a 3.1-cubic-foot two-door mini fridge or an 8-by-10-inch rug in pinks and creams. I recommend entering these items in a shared cloud spreadsheet.

Once you have the list, you can use one of these three methods to divide the costs.

1. Assign rough costs to each item and split the list so each roommate's total is about equal (preferred).
2. If one student really prefers to do all the shopping, you can split the cost evenly, but please decide before move-in who will take responsibility for storing, donating, or recycling each item at the end of the school year.
3. If these methods don't work for some reason, you can consider an owner model in which the roommates who didn't purchase the item pay a small "use fee" for the year. This can get messy, though, so I would suggest using one of the above methods instead.

Take a photo of the final version of the cloud sheet just in case it gets lost, and save it in everyone's phones.

Key Actions to Take

- [ ] Follow "Class of" or Accepted Students accounts for your school.
- [ ] Go through the seven compatibility matching topics on pages 72–74 and answer them honestly. If you're comfortable, share your answers with a close friend or family member and see if they agree.
- [ ] Start a shared spreadsheet for shared items and take a first pass at your list, being careful to follow all school rules and requirements.
- [ ] Consider sending your roommate(s) a copy of this book so you'll all be on the same page. 😊

7

Dorm Beds

Choose the Height, Then Layer for Comfort

What You'll Take Away

- An understanding of the different dorm bed heights
- How to layer a dorm bed and what not to do
- What size, materials, and certifications to look for in each bed layer
- Where it's smart to splurge and where you can save

Your bed is, without a doubt, the most important area of the dorm room: It's where you'll sleep, study, lounge, scroll, and sometimes even eat. But before you can make it cozy, you have to understand what you're working with: bed heights, thin mattresses, and limited flexibility. This chapter breaks down everything you need to know about setting up a dorm bed that's both comfortable and practical, from what layers actually matter to where it's worth spending a little extra.

Pro Tip: Dorm beds take up the most real estate in a dorm room; a twin XL bed is about 22 square feet.

UNDERSTANDING BED HEIGHTS (AND RISERS)

Before we get into bed heights, let's take a look at a typical adjustable dorm bed.

There are only a handful of companies that manufacture dorm beds, so there are variations, but they're all pretty similar: a headboard, a footboard, and a metal spring deck.

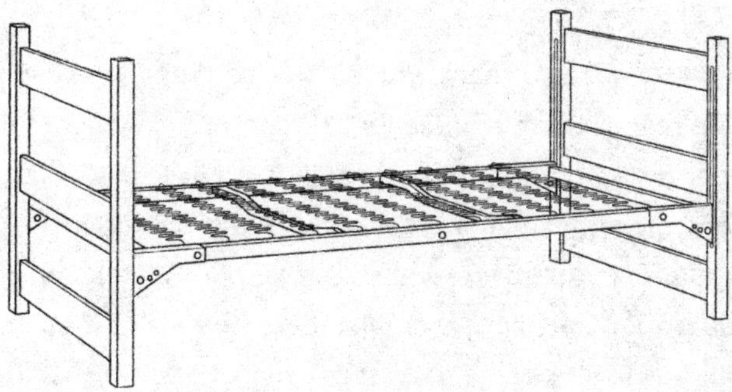

A typical regular height dorm bed frame with the metal spring deck (the horizontal platform that the mattress sits on). The slots in each of the four legs have pegs to hold the spring deck at different heights.

Some schools have metal beds, and some schools provide beds that aren't adjustable, but most are wood with slats or holes in the legs that allow the spring deck to be raised and lowered to different heights.

Generally, there are three dorm bed varieties, and each school may have only one consistent variety, or it may vary by building or room type. The dorm bed manufacturers do not consistently name these styles, but I'll use these bed height names throughout the book for consistency:

1. **Regular height**—34 to 36 inches high (shown in the illustration above), with an adjustable bed deck height. These beds can sometimes be bunked with school-provided hardware or lofted with a school-provided loft kit or a loft kit available from the school's approved provider/installer.
2. **Junior loft**—54 to 60 inches high, with an adjustable bed deck height. A bed rail should be used.
3. **Fully lofted**—69 to 73 inches high, with an adjustable bed deck height. A bed rail should be used.

Pro Tip: Why do so many students raise their regular-height beds up higher than a typical bed? For storage, of course! Remember that most double dorm rooms are 150 to 200 square feet, of which only half is "your side." Typically, you have 75 to 100 square feet of space, and a twin XL bed will take up about 22 square feet. Raising a regular-height dorm bed up to the highest level will give you about 30 inches of clearance below your 22-square-foot bed for storage.

Depending on the bed that is used by your school and the rules for raising and lofting, you may have up to six height options for your dorm bed:

1. **Low:** Mattress at the lowest position, similar to as on beds at home, with very little storage space below. If the head of the bed is not up against the wall, a headboard will let you lean back and keep your pillows on the bed.
2. **Mid-Height:** If you don't need a lot of storage space below the bed, this is a nice height as you won't need an ottoman/footstool (or a running start) to get up to your bed.
3. **Raised Height (aka Captain's Height or Semi-Lofted):** The very top setting of a regular-height bed, this height provides 28 to 32 inches of clearance below for storage, but it will require a footstool or ottoman to get up to the bed once you add your bed layers. Many schools have three-drawer dressers that fit perfectly under a raised-height bed.
4. **Junior Loft:** About 54 inches of clearance below the bed is not enough to be able to stand underneath it, but you can put a desk or seating below the bed. This is a taller head/footboard than raised height but not as tall as fully lofted.
5. **Fully Lofted:** Up high, similar to a top bunk but with a lot of open space underneath for a desk or a lounge space. With about 70 inches of clearance below the bed, many students are able to stand underneath it.
6. **Bunked:** One bed over another, with similar rail/clearance concerns as lofts.

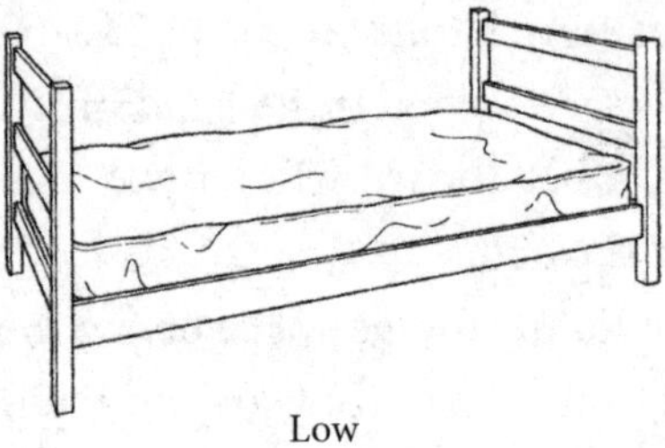

Low

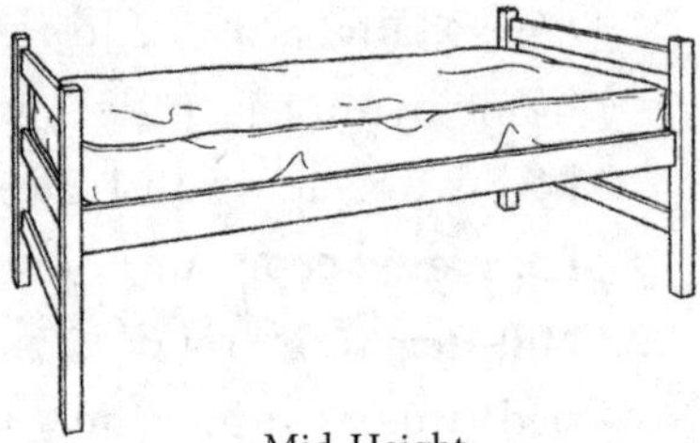

Mid-Height

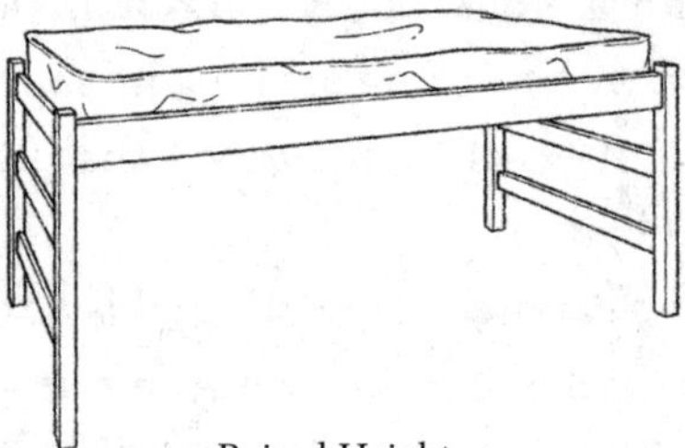

Raised Height

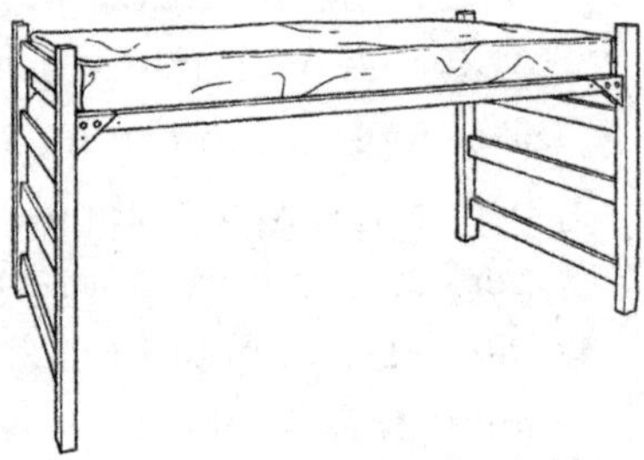

Junior Loft

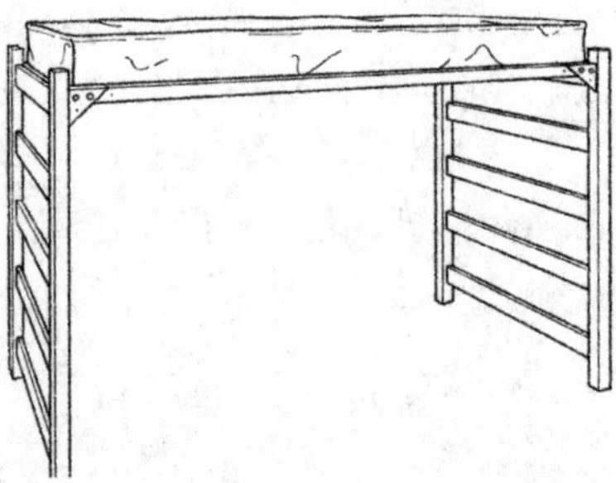

Fully Lofted

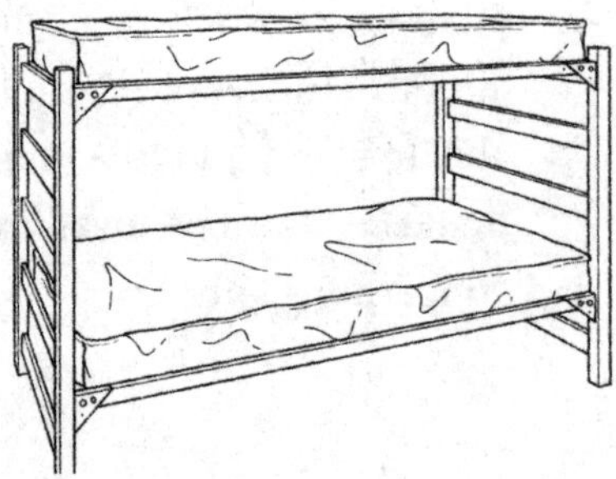

Bunked

The six typical dorm bed heights. Some schools may have other options.

How to Adjust the Height of a Regular-Height Dorm Bed

Adjusting the height of your bed might seem like a big task, but it's actually pretty simple. I raise and lower my dorm beds at home easily, but you'll definitely want two people to prevent accidents or injuries. Here's how to proceed.

1. **Check with your RA.** Some colleges have specific regulations or require that maintenance staff make height adjustments.
2. **Get set up.** Have a rubber mallet at the ready! If you are permitted to adjust the bed yourself, adhere to the school's guidelines for doing so safely, and remove the mattress first.
3. **Adjust the bed.** Use the rubber mallet to nudge the horizontal rails out of their slots and reset them at the desired height.

If your dorm bed is adjustable and you are also allowed to use risers, I would try to get by without them. The exception to this is if there is no other spot for a mini fridge; then you'll need the bed to be up at least 32 inches for most 3-cubic-foot fridges.

What If Your Dorm Doesn't Have Adjustable Beds?

Some schools do not provide adjustable beds. Bed risers have long been the answer, if they're permitted! Back in the day, students used cinder blocks to raise their beds, but the turn of the century brought purpose-built bed risers made specifically for those boxy dorm bed legs.

Here's what you need to know about bed risers.

- You must check school policies—bed risers are on several prohibited lists. If they are permitted, there might be height limits (often 6 or 8 inches).
- Check the foot of the bed and match the riser design—square

posts, tubular legs, or solid panels across the back. There are risers for all three; just be sure to pay attention to the bed style before purchasing.

Should You Fully Loft Your Dorm Bed?

If you are permitted to loft your dorm bed, you may wonder if you *should*. Good question—here are pros and cons that I've found over the years.

Pros:

- **Extra Living Space:** Ideal for maximizing under-bed space. Use the space as a lounge (with a futon or comfortable chair) under one bed and a TV and kitchen space (mini fridge, microwave, food storage) under the other. You could also move the desks below the lofted beds to free up other space in the room.
- **Privacy Boost:** Offers a bit more privacy for sleeping. Some have even installed curtain panels below the bed to create a more private place to study or hang out.
- **Room Layout Flexibility:** Enables far more creative dorm room arrangements when you can move some furniture below the bed.

Cons:

- **Climbing, Always Climbing:** Climbing up and down multiple times a day can be inconvenient.
- **Limited Headroom:** Sleep space can feel cramped in rooms with low ceilings.
- **Reduced Bedside Storage and Access:** While there are attached bedside tables that can be added to a higher bed, you lose the

option for a full nightstand and more items within arm's reach when you sleep up high.

- **Safety Concerns:** Higher beds have increased fall risks. Please be sure the bed comes with a bed rail or bring your own safety rail.

Safety Tip: Bed safety rails should be mandatory at all colleges, but unfortunately they are not. If you will have a lofted bed, and the school or third party cannot provide a safety rail, please bring your own. It must be at least 5 inches above the top of the sleeping surface (mattress plus bedding).

How Do You Fully Loft a Dorm Bed?

When I was in college, an army of dads showed up with lumber and drills to build a loft bed frame, but today's safety standards no longer allow this, although there may be a rare exception. If dorm beds are allowed to be fully lofted at your school, you'll likely need to do one of the following:

- Submit a work order to have them raised or installed.
- Order a loft kit from the school's approved third-party supplier. This will likely require a rental fee, but the kit should be set up and waiting for you on move-in day.

In either situation, check the deadlines for submitting these requests, as the school may not be able to accommodate last-minute requests.

How Do You Get Up to a Fully Lofted Bed?

If you fully loft your bed or are in an upper bunk, how do you get up there? If you are lucky, there will be a ladder. Most of the time, you will need to crawl up to the higher beds using the slats on the headboard or footboard.

Some students will place their desk or dresser next to those slats and step on that piece of furniture before continuing up the slats.

> **Pro Tip:** Those wooden bed slats can be uncomfortable on bare feet. Use 18-inch pieces of round pipe insulation (from a home improvement store) with a pre-cut slit to slip over the slats. Secure the insulation in place with zip ties on the outer ends.

THE LAYERS OF A DORM BED

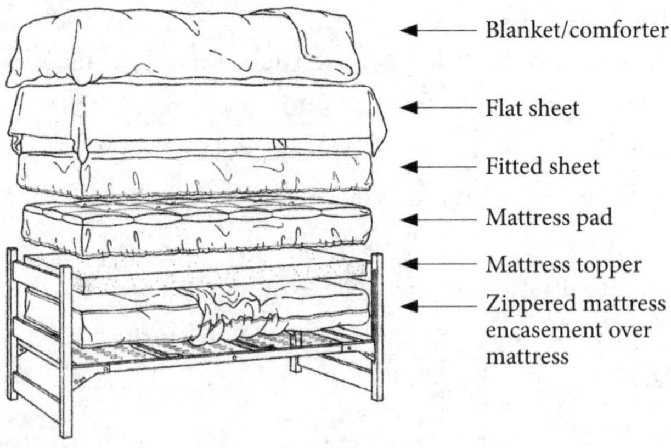

How to layer a dorm bed to make the industrial mattress more comfortable.

When I started researching dorm essentials in 2021, I never dreamed that there was an art to layering a dorm bed. But when you combine an uncomfortable vinyl mattress with typically warm, humid dorm rooms, a comfortable yet cooling solution is needed!

Most dorm beds have industrial, hard, vinyl-covered mattresses averaging 5 to 8 inches thick, with the majority at 6 inches. For comparison, most mattresses in your home are 10 to 16 inches thick.

I developed a simple graphic explaining how to properly layer a dorm bed, and it became internet-famous in short order because there are so many questions about this topic every year.

Before the how, let's define the mattress product terms so we're speaking the same language.

It is easy to confuse these five products because many of us use the terms interchangeably. Even the manufacturers are inconsistent in naming products. I include the first three in the dorm bed layering plan, but here is how I distinguish among all five:

- **Mattress Encasement:** A six-sided, zippered cover that completely encloses the mattress for full hygiene and pest protection; typically thin and not a comfort layer.
- **Mattress Topper:** A thick comfort layer (often 2 to 4 inches) placed on top of the mattress to change the feel. Toppers typically add pressure relief and either more softness or more support. Some mattress toppers come with their own cover.
- **Mattress Pad:** A quilted, lightly cushioned layer that lies on top of the mattress or mattress topper (usually like a fitted bottom sheet) to add minor comfort and a washable buffer.
- **Mattress Protector:** A thin five-sided fitted cover (bottom open) with a waterproof/breathable barrier that shields the mattress from spills, sweat, and allergens. It is more like a thick sheet and adds little to no cushioning.

- **Mattress Cover:** A generic umbrella term retailers use for any cover. It can refer to a protector or an encasement or the removable fabric cover on a mattress topper. If you're considering a product called a mattress cover, always check whether it's five-sided (a protector) or six-sided (an encasement).

HOW TO LAYER YOUR DORM BED

This is how to layer from the dorm-provided mattress up:

1. Tight-fitting zippered encasement around the dorm mattress (optional)
2. Mattress topper
3. Fitted-sheet-style mattress pad if the topper does not have a removable, washable cover
4. Regular-pocket, fully elasticized fitted sheet
5. Flat sheet (this is optional since today's teenagers often skip this in favor of a soft blanket layer)
6. Blanket/comforter/duvet (how many or what type is a matter of personal preference; keep it similar to what is used at home)

Let's go through each layer: why it is important, what size to use, and what to look for in each when shopping.

1. Zippered Mattress Encasement

Purpose

An encasement is an optional layer that many choose to include to seal off the used dorm mattress from their own bedding. Alternatively (or additionally), bring disinfecting wipes to wipe down the entire mattress on move-in day before making the bed.

Size

- The encasement should be the exact size of the mattress.
- It is important to use a low-profile encasement meant for thinner mattresses. If you put a mattress encasement meant for a 14-inch-deep mattress on a 6-inch-deep mattress, all that extra fabric will bunch up and likely cause your topper above to shift around while you sleep.

What to Look For

- **Nontoxic Certification:** Choose an encasement that is OEKO-TEX certified to ensure that it contains no harmful chemicals.
- **Closure:** Ensure there is a continuous zipper with a zip guard or Velcro at the end to seal.
- **Bedbug Protection:** Just about all encasements have this, but it is not typically necessary for a vinyl-covered dorm mattress. However, if you have a regular mattress (not bedbug-proof and not cleanable) in a dorm or apartment, I highly recommend a mattress encasement to keep that mattress separate from you and your bedding.
- **Waterproofing:** This is useful for spills but not completely necessary since this will be under your topper and mattress pad, plus there is no need to protect the vinyl-covered mattress from liquids.
- **Care:** Opt for machine-washable if possible, but at a minimum, check max water temp and drying instructions.

What Not to Do

- Do not put the mattress topper inside the encasement with the mattress. Some people recommend doing this, but all the topper manufacturers warn against it. Encasements are airtight, but foam toppers need to breathe and let heat escape. If heat builds up, moisture can form in the topper, potentially leading to mold development. I have seen this happen myself—you do not want to foster that environment.

2. Mattress Topper

Purpose

Thick and typically foam, a mattress topper adds comfort to the vinyl-covered, thin, springy dorm mattress.

Size

- The topper should be the exact same size as the mattress. You can use a smaller topper if you are okay with the entire mattress not being covered, but if possible, match the mattress size.
- Memory foam mattress toppers range from 2 to 4 inches thick, and bigger is not always better—the thinner the topper, the more firm, and the thicker, the more squishy and sink-in.
    - 2-inch-thick mattress toppers are good for those who like a firm sleep surface or who will be in an upper bunk or fully lofted bed with limited clearance below the ceiling.
    - 3-inch-thick mattress toppers provide medium support and are the top choice for most students.
    - 4-inch-thick mattress toppers are soft and plush, but many students report that they are too soft and make it difficult to roll over. Some love them, though, especially those used to sleeping on softer surfaces.

What to Look For

- **Nontoxic Certification:** Select only CertiPUR-US certified memory foam toppers to ensure that there are no harmful substances in the topper. Toppers accurately labeled with this certification will not give off that toxic smell when opened or need days to "air out."
- **Gel:** Most memory foam toppers have this important ingredient. Gel helps pull heat away from the body, allowing the foam to stay cooler. This doesn't guarantee cool sleep, but it will help. Heat needs to be released, which is why I warned against putting your topper inside a mattress encasement in the previous section.
- **Cover:** Some foam toppers, especially the more premium models, include a removable, washable cover. These covers are breathable and allow heat to escape from the foam topper inside. In addition to the protection a cover provides, I find it adds structure to the topper and helps the bed feel more like sleeping on a typical mattress.
- **Straps:** Some foam toppers with covers include elastic straps in the corners to go around the mattress. Sliding mattress toppers are a common complaint of college students, and the straps help keep the topper in place.
- **Care:** Memory foam cannot be laundered. After a long school year, sprinkle your topper with baking soda and allow it to sit in the sun for several hours on a dry day. Lightly vacuum or sweep up the remaining baking soda.

What Not to Do

- Do not buy an uncertified foam mattress topper.
- Do not put a foam mattress topper inside an airtight mattress encasement.

3. Mattress Pad

Purpose

A quilted mattress pad over the mattress topper provides light cushioning, adds a washable buffer, and helps keep the layers below in place.

Size

- The mattress pad must be the same size as the mattress.
- Ideally, the mattress pad would be made for mattresses up to 12 inches deep, but these are hard to find. You don't need deep pockets—you want snug elastic helping to hold the layers in place.

What to Look For

- **Style:** You want a fitted-sheet-style mattress pad with a fully elasticized skirt. Avoid corner-only elastic.
- **Fabric:** 100 percent cotton or percale will be cooler than microfiber, polyester, or "down-alternative" materials.
- **Nontoxic Certification:** OEKO-TEX certified.
- **Waterproofing:** I have a love/hate relationship with waterproof mattress pads. I love that they protect your mattress topper from sweat and spills, but they can be warm and noisy. The waterproof layer is a heat generator, so unless it's absolutely

necessary, I recommend a thicker, non-waterproof mattress pad.

- **Breathability:** The sides of fitted-sheet-style mattress pads are breathable and often semi-sheer, allowing toppers below to let heat escape.
- **Care:** Machine-washable.

What Not to Do

- Purchase a deep-pocket mattress pad.

4. Sheets (Fitted and Optional Flat)

Purpose

I think we all know what bedsheets are, but the fitted bottom sheet in particular is an important layer that helps hold the topper in place. The material is important for sleep temperature.

Size

- The fitted sheet must be the same size as the mattress.
- A flat sheet is optional—an increasing number of today's college students don't use one. You can buy twin XL and other size fitted sheets separately.
- Your thin 5-to-8-inch dorm mattress plus a 2-to-4-inch topper brings the total depth to 7 to 12 inches. Deep-pocket sheets are not necessary; in fact, if the fitted sheet is too loose, it won't be as helpful in holding your topper in place.

What to Look For

- **Style:** It is very important to ensure that fitted sheets have a fully elasticized skirt, not just elastic in the corners.

Corner-only elastic will almost certainly allow the sheets to pop off easily.

- **Fabric and Weave:** While microfiber (a fancy word for polyester) sheets are very soft and inexpensive, they run warm. In addition to the heat factor, microfiber tends to stretch out and lose its shape quickly. This does not help with holding the layers in place. For this reason, I recommend only 100 percent cotton sheets for college. Cotton comes in many different weaves, but these are the most common for college:
  - **For a cooler feel:** Percale is the most breathable, is moisture-wicking, and feels more crisp, similar to hotel sheets.
  - **For a cozier feel:** Sateen is a denser weave that feels more luxurious but is a little warmer. Sateen drapes better than percale.
  - **For warmth:** If the dorm turns out to be chilly, 100 percent cotton flannel or jersey weaves will add warmth.
- **Pocket Depth:** Unless you have a dorm mattress over 8 inches thick, stick with a regular pocket.
- **Nontoxic Certification:** OEKO-TEX certified.
- **Care:** Machine-washable.
- **Bonus:** Look for sheets with extra elastic on the corners to help the sheets stay in place.

NOTE: While most dorm rooms run warm and somewhat damp, don't count on your dorm building temperatures to be in line with the climate. Some dorm rooms are absolutely freezing when the air-conditioning is on, while others at the other end of the hall may be too warm because they're on the "far end" of the vent system. The same goes for heat in the winter. It is best to get information directly from the school or from students who have recently lived in your dorm building.

5. Top Layers (Blanket/Comforter /Duvet)

Purpose

Warmth and a finished look. Keep in mind that beds in a dorm room are used not only for sleeping but frequently also as a lounge space, study space, and even a dining area. Choose a sturdy, machine-washable top layer.

Size

Here is where you have flexibility if you have a twin or twin XL bed. Your blankets and comforter layers can be larger than the provided mattress size. There are pros and cons of using actual size and larger sizes, as explained in the table below.

Consideration	Twin or Twin XL Size	Full or Queen Size
Fit	Often combined into one size offering. Look for at least 88 inches in length for a twin XL bed.	Often combined into one size offering. Look for at least 88 inches in length for a twin XL bed.
Comfort	Easy to kick off or remove if the room is warm.	Can feel too warm and difficult to remove mid-sleep.
Storage Screen	Will cover the mattress but not the storage below.	Will cover some of the storage below.
Frustration Factor	Easier to launder and make the bed with.	Harder to launder and may more easily slide off the bed due to a weight imbalance on one side.
Reusability	As many off-campus housing options include full or queen beds, twin/twin XL bedding may not be reusable.	Reusable in dorm or off-campus living.
Cost	Typically less expensive than larger sizes but may command a premium late in the dorm shopping season.	Typically more expensive than twin XL bedding; the amount will differ by style and seller.

What to Look For

- **Warmth Level:** Consider personal sleep preferences as well as building temperatures. Layering a lightweight blanket with a comforter allows for flexibility.
- **Nontoxic Certification:** OEKO-TEX certified.
- **Care:** Machine-washable.

What about bed skirts?

Those looking for a more finished look to their room often use a bed skirt (on regular-height beds only, not fully lofted beds) to cover the area under their beds.

In order to select bed skirts, you'll need to know the clearance from the bottom of the spring deck to the floor.

You can purchase dorm-length bed skirts made specifically for raised dorm beds. You can also DIY your own using fabric, window treatment panels, shower curtains, or bedsheets. Use zip ties to attach these to your bed frame.

There are adjustable dorm bed skirts that use ties that can be attached toward the front or the back of the mattress springs, allowing you to position them for the length you choose.

WHERE TO SPLURGE VERSUS WHERE TO SAVE

Items that are splurge-worthy (based on comfort and/or reusability):

- **Mattress Topper:** The topper can make or break comfort, and sleep is so important in college. Consider the number of years of use before splurging.

- **100 Percent Cotton Sheets:** Cooler, thicker, and less likely to stretch out and lose their shape.
- **Comforter:** If you'll be using the same size for multiple years, will care for it properly, and aren't one to redecorate due to trends.

Save on these bedding items:

- **Comforter:** If you'll have only one year in this bed size, spend sparingly on the top layer.
- **Mattress Pad:** As long as it has a fully elasticized skirt and is OEKO-TEX certified, it does not need to be expensive.
- **Extra Throws and Pillows:** Nice to have, but they are difficult to store when it is time to sleep.

KEEP IN MIND: Dorm life, especially freshman year, is a big change for students. Being on their own for the first time with busy schedules and evolving social lives means that cleaning often takes a backseat. Factor this into where to save and where to splurge. Comforters and sheets live a hard year, so affordable, durable, machine-washable bedding is best.

Key Actions to Take

- ☐ **Learn your bed height options and discuss ideas with your roommate, especially if you're considering lofting and shared lounge space below.**
- ☐ **Understand the measurements of your bed—frame size, mattress thickness, guardrail height, ceiling clearance—and check housing rules (regarding risers, height adjustments),**

then plan your bedding setup using the guide above.

- ☐ Get comfortable with laundry: If the student does not yet handle their laundry (including bedding), they should start practicing now so that it is routine by move-in.

8

Storage Strategies & Protecting Valuables

What You'll Take Away

- → A list of what typically needs a "home" in a dorm room (beyond clothes)
- → Variables that will impact your storage options
- → How to keep valuables, medications, and important documents safe
- → Suggested ground rules around shared spaces, visitors, and valuables
- → A nudge to label and document your belongings

You've seen the Instagram-worthy dorm move-in day photos, but have you ever seen a photo of a dorm room a few weeks *after* move-in? There is a reason those don't make their way to social media!

Keeping things neat is difficult in a room with just a small closet, a desk, and a short dresser for storage. The goal here is to come up with a realistic storage plan and a list of items you'll need to bring to help make sure everything has a place.

This chapter provides guidelines for your storage plan, including how to keep valuables and personal items safe. The following chapters are a deeper dive into the places where you can generate some storage space—under the bed, in the closet, on the desk, and potentially in a small kitchen area.

VARIABLES THAT IMPACT YOUR STORAGE OPTIONS

In case you've skipped right to this chapter, let me highlight things that can impact your storage plan so you can get the answers you need to help you plan.

- Housing rules
- Dorm room layout
- Provided furniture
- Bed height
- Closet type
- Doors and over-door clearance
- Bathroom location

As you learned in chapter 1, every campus has its own rules, room layouts, furniture types, and sizes. You may not know the exact measurements, but you can create a general storage plan for your room once you have a dorm assignment. Some of the school-specific rules or layouts that may impact your storage plans include:

- Whether outside furniture is permitted (and what is considered furniture)

- Bed height options
- Limitations on over-door use
- Limitations on placing items near windows or wall air vents, which are often under the windows
- Bathroom location and setup (down the hall or attached with some storage)
- Type of closet and available space
- Built-in furniture, shelves, or in-room cabinets

WHAT WILL YOU NEED TO STORE?

Clothes and shoes are a big consideration in the plan. In addition to everyday clothes, you might need business attire for meetings, interviews, and banquets. You may also need cocktail or formalwear for formals; workout clothes for that awesome rec center on campus; and rain or cold-weather gear. Depending on where you go to school, it adds up.

Remember not to overdo it. When asked at the end of the year what really wasn't necessary to bring to their dorm room, students and their parents agree—don't bring so many clothes.

In addition to storage for everyday clothes and shoes, you'll need storage for items such as:

- Off-season clothes, shoes, and outerwear
- Game day wear and accessories
- Food, snacks, and drinks plus dishes, mugs, water bottles, and silverware
- Possibly a few small appliances with accessories like coffee pods or microwave cooking accessories
- Toiletries plus backstock
- School supplies

- First aid items, over-the-counter drugs, and prescription medications
- Jewelry and accessories
- Technology and accessories (chargers, charging cables, batteries, external drives, headphones)
- Laundry and cleaning supplies
- Extra towels and linens
- Extra paper products (paper towels, toilet paper, tissues)
- Gear for your hobby, sport, or major (musical instruments, sports equipment, lab goggles, studio supplies, art materials)

Simple, flexible, and inexpensive storage solutions are best. Remember, your storage solutions should make your life easier, not create more clutter to manage.

To help decide what goes where, use these three criteria:

1. Daily-use items should be within standing or sitting reach.
2. Weekly-use items can be a little farther from reach.
3. Seasonal or backstock items can be at step stool height or at the back of the under-bed storage.

MAXIMIZING STORAGE SPACE

As discussed on page 84, you'll be lucky to have 100 square feet for your side of the room, and in that space will be your bed (22 square feet), closet, desk, and dresser.

You've got an understanding of the room layout and dorm rules and a list of what you'll need to store. How will you fit it all in your part of the room?

The best approach is using vertical space through a strategy I refer to as space stacking.

Under-Bed Storage

The area under the bed is the biggest space for storage, especially if you raise or loft the bed. If you have 30 inches of clearance below your bed frame and choose 21-inch-tall drawers, that won't maximize your space. But if you absolutely have to have those 21-inch-tall drawers, consider adding bins to stack on top of them that are about 8 inches tall. Every little bit helps, because there are lots of small items that will need a home.

Go Vertical

You can't create more floor space, but you can go up for more stacking! You could:

- Add a hutch with cubbies on your desk.
- Use an 18-by-24-inch shelving rack over your mini fridge—one of my favorite ways to create space.
- Stack storage inside the closet.
- Consider over-the-door storage and also using the inside of closet doors.
- Fill the space between the heads of the beds if you have a typical parallel bed layout.

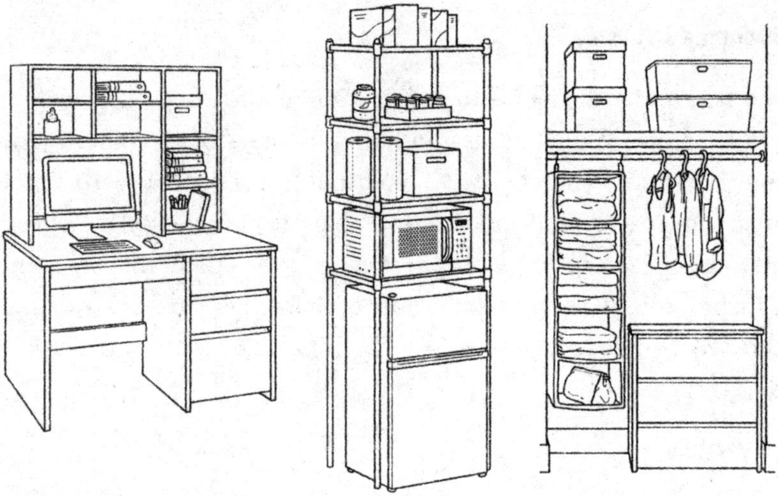

Examples of creating vertical storage (from left to right): a desk hutch, a vertical dorm kitchen, and closet storage above and below the clothes hanging area.

Prevent Losing and Misplacing Items

Keys, lanyards, headphones, glasses, lip balm, remotes, charging blocks and cables—set aside a small drawer, add a few wall hooks, or designate a bin to catch these items as they come into the room or are used during the day. It is amazing how small things can disappear even in a small dorm room.

KEEP YOUR BELONGINGS SAFE

Many people assume that since your dorm room door locks and your roommate seems trustworthy, your belongings inside your room are protected.

The biggest concerns about theft come with the door being left open when friends visit or when you run down the hall to ask a neighbor about something. Or maybe your roommate has new friends stop by when you are not in the room. Laptops, gaming devices, and other small electronics can be quickly and quietly removed.

I've read several accounts of theft and even "excessive borrowing." One roommate had to keep her premium-brand leggings locked away because her roommate kept taking them and then insisting they were hers all along.

Safety Tip: As with other situations, if you see something, say something. Petty theft can be an issue on college campuses, but if incidents or concerns are quickly reported, cameras and other security measures may solve those cases quickly and prevent future theft.

A member of our community reported that their school had a string of incidents where young thieves posing as students would lurk outside the dorm waiting for a resident to walk out and then slip into the building before the door closed and locked again. They then proceeded through the halls looking for open or unlocked doors.

Hopefully, you won't encounter situations like this, but it is a good idea to safely store your personal items.

What to Keep in Locked Storage

It is always a good practice to leave family heirlooms and irreplaceable items that you'd be heartbroken to lose safely at home, but in addition to valuables, important documents such as social security cards, passports, and birth certificates need to be kept secure. You may not need to bring these items to college, but if you plan to get a job or travel while in school, you may need to have them in the dorm room at some point.

Prescription medications also need secure storage. For refrigerated medications, request approval to have your own mini fridge that you can secure from the outside; otherwise, use a refrigerator-safe locking box inside a shared fridge.

Locking your valuables isn't about distrust; it is about protection for those moments when the dorm room door is propped open, or was accidentally left unlocked. Consider keeping the following items in locked storage in your dorm room:

- **Electronics**—Laptops, iPads, gaming systems, and AirPods.
- **Credit and Debit Cards, Gift Cards, and Cash**—Your student ID should work as a "credit card" on campus, so you generally shouldn't need to carry cash or cards with you unless you're leaving campus.
- **Jewelry**—Any pieces that look real should be safeguarded. I recommend not bringing the diamond earrings from Grandma to the dorm.
- **Textbooks**—It may sound strange to mention textbooks, but some specialty textbooks can cost $250 and up to purchase and are easily resold for hundreds of dollars, so they can be easy targets.
- **Important Documents**—If you must bring an original social security card, birth certificate, passport, or passport card, keep these locked up safely.
- **Medication**—Controlled substances used for ADHD, anxiety, and pain are among the top items stolen from dorm rooms.

If you plan to bring a bike to college, please do your research on the best way to secure your bike when not in use. Consider placing a hidden tracking device on the bike, and look into registering it with the school or with campus police.

Locking Storage for Dorm Rooms

Before you add locking storage to your shopping list, check your dorm-provided furniture closely. Some dorms have a desk drawer with a lock or a lockable wardrobe unit or dresser drawer. If there are actual closet doors, these may have locks. Each of these should have unique keys for each student.

You may be thinking, "Wouldn't someone just pick up a safe and walk away with the whole thing?" Excellent question.

For each of the recommendations below, use a cable lock to tether the safe to a stationary object in the dorm room such as your bed frame or bed rail. Just make sure that the locking storage you choose has a handle or other way to wrap a cable lock through it.

Common Safes or Locking Storage Used for College

Small lockbox	Good for flat items like a wallet, credit or gift cards, a passport, and earbuds.
Medicine lockbox	Made specifically to handle the depth of a bottle or several bottles.
Larger safe	There are options that will hold a laptop, medications, and small items as well as important documents. Some of these come with a tethered locking cable.
Footlocker with padlock	If you need larger storage, perhaps for a gaming console as well as other electronics and valuables, most footlockers come with openings for a padlock. You can add your own padlock and thread a cable lock through it and around your bed rail to keep it in the room.

Room Access and Roommate Etiquette

As part of your roommate agreement, include stipulations for locking the door even for short periods away from the room. Agree to keep guests from handling any of the roommate's personal items or opening drawers or closets. Be clear that no medication is to be shared and that no items are to be borrowed without permission.

LABEL AND RECORD VALUABLES

It may seem like an early elementary school tactic to label items, but it just makes sense. So many students have similar phone chargers, water bottles, personal technology, small appliances, clothes, and backpacks.

You don't have to put bright white labels on everything, but at least use a permanent marker to write your name on the wall side of your charging blocks and on the bottom of calculators, gaming consoles, personal technology, and water bottles. Draw a unique line around your charging cables, and add your initials to your clothing labels and the inside of your expensive slippers and shoes.

In the section on move-in day planning on page 258, I'll explain how I recommend documenting your belongings. Make sure to include photos of your valuables, jewelry, electronics, and anything you feel needs to be documented such as an expensive jacket, golf clubs, or musical instruments. Those should all be labeled too! As an additional security measure, document or photograph the serial numbers on all electronic devices. Store these in the cloud.

CONSIDER DORM INSURANCE

Dorm insurance is quite inexpensive and something to consider to cover all your dorm room belongings including clothing, electronics, jewelry, and other valuables. While your homeowner's insurance may cover a short-term dorm residence, I recommend considering a separate policy for a dorm room. The deductible should be lower, and any dorm claims will not contribute toward raising your home insurance premiums.

Key Actions to Take

- ☐ Research the list of variables for your school to understand your storage options.
- ☐ Make a general list of the items you'll bring and determine a room location for each.
- ☐ Determine if your school has locking storage in the dorm rooms or if you'll need to bring your own.
- ☐ Start labeling valuables and clothes that are definitely going to college.
- ☐ Look into dorm insurance costs.

9

Plan & Maximize Under-Bed Storage

What You'll Take Away

- How to measure the exact space below the dorm bed in order to plan for storage
- An understanding of the "front" space and the "back" space
- Storage options that work well under dorm beds

This chapter is specific to planning for storage below a regular-height bed, usually set at the highest level, often called captain's height. If you loft your bed high enough to place furniture below, such as your desk or seating, your storage planning shifts to other parts of the room (see chapter 14).

The largest storage space in a dorm room is typically under the bed, which can be raised by either adjusting the height or adding risers. It may seem like chaos, but I have a method to both maximize and organize this important storage area. You'll start by calculating the available space, determining what needs to be stored below the bed, and selecting the types of storage for both the "front" and the "back" of the space.

The "front" of the under-bed space is the storage visible from the room. The "back" is the storage behind the front storage, usually up against the wall.

DETERMINE THE AVAILABLE SPACE BELOW THE BED

To maximize the storage area, you'll need to know the length, width, and height of the area below the bed. The bed location is helpful to know but not required at this point. If the bed will not be up against a wall, you'll have the benefit of being able to easily access both sides of the storage space.

Use the size of your mattress as your blueprint for storage space. Below are the measurements (width and length) of standard mattress sizes. Many dorm beds are twin XL, but I also see twin setups, and full and full XL are becoming more prevalent every year.

- Twin: 38 by 75 inches
- Twin XL: 38 by 80 inches
- Full: 54 by 75 inches
- Full XL: 54 by 80 inches
- Queen: 60 by 80 inches

Plan on your available storage space being about the same size space as the mattress; the bed frame should be just outside the mattress perimeter. You'll also need to determine how high you will adjust the bed to know the maximum height of one or stacked storage organizers.

Clearance Below the Bed Frame

Clearance is the height from the floor to the horizontal bed rail where your mattress rests. The height of any storage below will need to be just under this height, whether one unit or stacked. To determine what you'll need:

1. Check the housing page for your dorm. Are the beds adjustable? Does the page list the max height and include the measurement to the floor? If you can't find this information, please refer to page 3 for suggestions about how to determine these measurements.
2. If the beds are not adjustable, does the housing page list the height between the bottom of the horizontal bed frame and the floor? Are risers permitted?

Most adjustable regular-height dorm beds raised to the highest level (captain's height) will have somewhere between 27 and 33 inches of clearance depending on the furniture and dorm rules.

If you're using risers, you'll have to do the math to determine your below-bed height for storage. Determine your bed clearance before using risers and then add the height of the risers. This is your total clearance.

If you'll have a twin XL bed with 30 inches of height in clearance, you'll have almost 53 cubic feet of storage space under that dorm bed! 80 × 38 × 30 ÷ 1,728 (12 × 12 × 12) = 52.8 cubic feet.

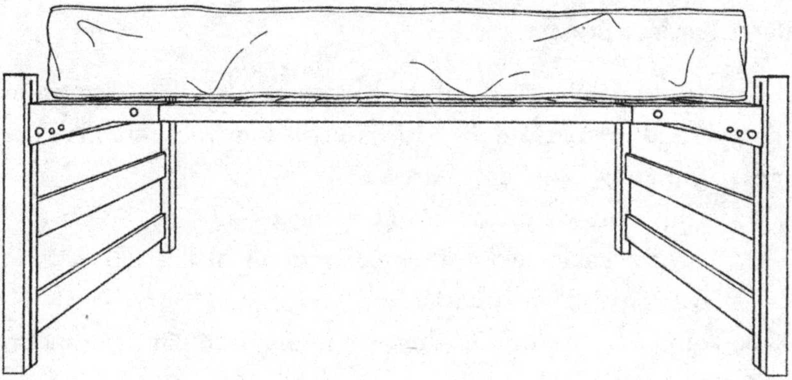

The typical twin XL adjustable dorm bed is 80 inches long and 38 to 40 inches wide, and a fully raised mattress will be 27 to 33 inches off the ground.

THE FRONT OF THE UNDER-BED SPACE (WHAT YOU SEE FROM THE ROOM)

There are some fairly standard options for the under-bed storage that faces the room. Most prefer for this storage to be neat and tidy, but before you spend time on the hunt, consider two things.

1. **Whether You'll Have a Bed Skirt**—If you plan to use a bed skirt to fully cover the space below the bed, the storage presentation becomes less important. Just remember that you'll need to hold up the bed skirt with one hand to reach under the bed.
2. **Comforter Size**—Instead of going with the full bed skirt solution, some choose to use a full/queen comforter, as discussed on page 99. This will cover approximately 12 inches of the storage below, leaving about 18 inches uncovered.

POPULAR UNDER-BED STORAGE SOLUTIONS

As with everything else I've discussed in this book, the dorm room and furniture variables will impact your storage layout.

Dorm-Provided Dresser

Before you start planning out the space under the bed, determine the style and size of the dorm-provided dresser. These are the three most commonly found dorm dressers:

1. A three-drawer dresser about 30 inches tall
2. Two stackable two-drawer dressers 18 inches tall each or 36 inches tall when stacked
3. A four- or five-drawer dresser ranging from 40 to 46 inches tall

The 30-inch dorm dressers usually fit perfectly under a fully raised adjustable regular-height dorm bed and are almost always 24 inches deep. Their width can vary from 24 to 36 inches. With a twin XL bed being 80 inches long, a 36-inch-wide dresser will take up nearly 50 percent of your "front" storage space.

Depending on the room layout, you may prefer to place the dresser in the room next to the desk, as the two should be the same height and depth, providing a continuous desk surface. Some small rooms can't accommodate this, though, and the only place to put the dresser is under the bed.

The 30-inch dressers may be stackable, too, if they don't fit or you'd rather them not be under the beds. Just be sure one of the roommates is tall enough to utilize the top drawer.

If each roommate is provided with two stackable two-drawer dressers, the additional storage space is nice, but these typically do not fit under the bed when stacked. If you place them side by side under the bed, they'll take up considerable horizontal space, so you'll want to stack the space above each set of drawers.

The taller four- or five-drawer dressers will fit only under a junior loft or fully lofted bed. Otherwise, they'll need a spot in the dorm room or in the closet, depending on the room layout and the closet's size. These dressers can often work well back-to-back with their sides up against the wall, and they're also a good spot to put a TV if you're bringing one to college.

Plastic Drawer Towers

Three-drawer storage towers typically come in two widths (13 or 22 inches) and are 25 inches tall and only about 16 inches deep. They are inexpensive, lightweight, and fairly sturdy as long as you don't fill the drawers with heavy objects.

Use these three-drawer towers to store clothes, extra linens, and first aid supplies, and to keep snacks out of sight. The best place to buy these is a big-box store. While you can find them at online-only retailers, they are usually much more expensive.

Pro Tip: If using plastic drawer towers in a space other than under the bed, you can pop the lid off one unit and stack a second on top. Further secure with zip ties around the back frame if desired.

Plastic drawer towers—two wide, one narrow—under a raised dorm bed.

Clear Plastic Drawer Carts

Inexpensive, lightweight, and mobile, these are great under desks without drawers or for extra storage space in shared bathrooms. If you need an extra flat surface now and then for a table or game space, consider the plastic drawers on casters that you can easily roll around the room. (Just be aware that the drawers are clear and don't conceal their contents.)

Pro Tip: Want to make it easy to access the "back" storage? Take two of these carts and secure them back-to-back with zip ties on the frames—just pull the drawers out slightly to wrap the zip ties around. Easily pull the unit out from under the bed and rotate to access the drawers on the other side!

Two plastic drawer carts under a raised dorm bed.

Plastic Clear Stacking Drawers

These come in various sizes and can be stacked and organized to meet your storage needs, holding everything from big, bulky sweaters to extra sets of sheets.

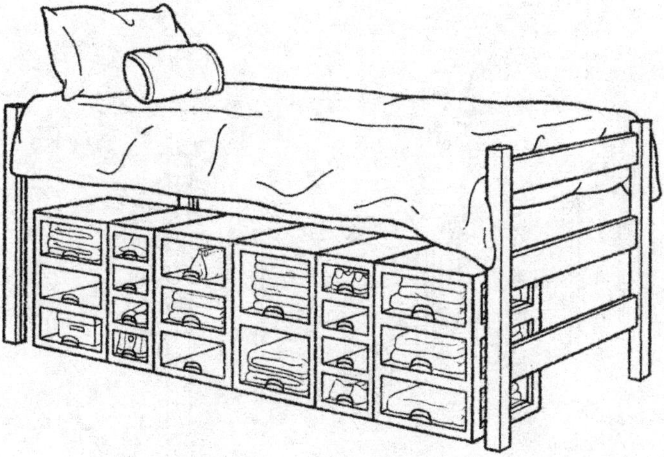

Clear stacking drawers in various sizes below a raised dorm bed.

Cube Organizers

Cube organizers with open spaces or bins look nice, but they are typically not very deep. If you go this route, consider having a strong plan for the back storage.

Cube organizers are available in two standard sizes—to fit 11-inch bins or 13-inch bins.

Pro Tip: The 13-inch cube organizers are far more sturdy and can hold about 20 percent more than the 11-inch versions.

You'll find cube organizers in many sizes and colors, and they can be placed horizontally or vertically. They are reusable in post-dorm life for apartment bedroom storage, TV stands, and even nightstands. I highly recommend the 13-inch size for longer-lasting, sturdier storage or as a base for media centers or mini kitchens (see page 155).

Two 13-inch four-cube organizers below a raised dorm bed.

Dressers with Fabric Drawers

Why don't students bring an additional wood dresser to place under their dorm bed with their dorm-provided dresser? I'll give you three reasons:

1. They are bulky and hard to fit in the car for move-in and move-out.
2. They are fairly heavy and hard to move.
3. They are more expensive than the other options and may not be as reusable once the student moves off-campus (non–dorm room beds just aren't this high).

Another increasingly popular option is metal-frame dressers with fabric drawers. Some schools do not allow fabric-drawer furniture, so please check the rules if you are considering this option.

These do tend to be a bit less deep than the drawer options discussed earlier, and they are also a bit more cumbersome to move

A pair of fabric-drawer dressers under a raised dorm bed.

with the metal frame. If you have the vehicle to move these, though, they are a good option to last throughout college as a storage solution in off-campus housing, too. Pay close attention to the height when shopping for fabric drawer dressers—they always look much taller in the photos than they actually are. You can pack the drawers full and tape them closed for moving.

A Catch-All Bin

A big factor in messy dorm rooms is not being sure where to put things coming into the room. A simple catch-all bin, with or without a lid, is a place for things to go when you don't know where else to put them. My boys appreciated this when people were coming over. It's an easy way to clean up quickly, until that bin suddenly overflows! I'd suggest something tall and narrow that will slip into any extra room under the bed. A regular routine to clean it out will prevent the black hole of lost items.

THE BACK OF THE UNDER-BED SPACE—THE USABLE STORAGE HIDDEN BEHIND THE NEATLY ORGANIZED FRONT

Many of the "front" under-bed storage options above are 12 to 18 inches deep. A twin or twin XL dorm bed is 38 inches deep, maybe 40 inches considering the frame, so that means more than half your space is still available behind your "front" room-facing storage.

The back is an ideal place to store off-season clothes, shoes, and bedding. Seasonal sports equipment, a suitcase, an inflatable mattress for overnight guests, and cases of sports drinks or bottled water also do well in that back space.

To store off-season bedding and clothes, you can use your moving bags or folding clothes storage bags—I like the ones with a plastic window so you'll know what's in each bag.

For overflow shoe storage, you can use under-bed shoe organizers or shoe shelves to keep less-used or off-season shoes out of the way.

On page 111, we discussed locking storage for valuables and personal items. The back under-bed section is a great place for these if you don't need to access them regularly. Keeping these items out of sight is always a great idea.

The dorm-provided desk chair is sometimes stored in the back under-bed space because some students opt to bring their own more comfortable desk chair and schools typically do not allow you to remove any of the provided furniture.

If one long side of the bed is not against a wall, you likely still won't see the "back" unless the room is set up for a triple or quad, but it will be easier to access.

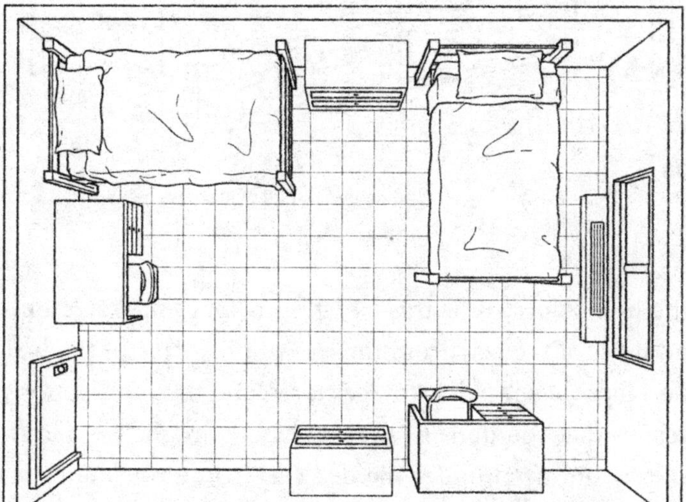

An overhead sketch of a room with one bed with no sides against the wall.

UNDER-BED STORAGE FOR LOW BEDS

Unfortunately, there are some situations where the beds are low, not adjustable, and risers are not permitted. You may then have only 8 to 14 inches of storage space under the bed. This may also be the case if you have bunk beds, as the lower bed has to be lower, and in this situation, you may have to share the space under the lower bed with your bunkmate.

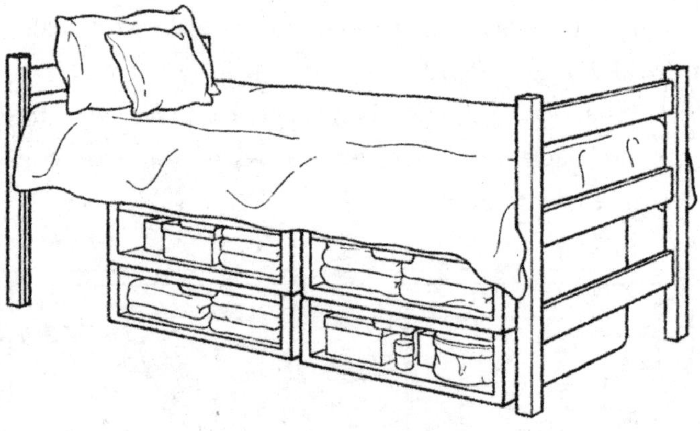

A low bed with stackable long, shallow drawers below.

The best solution for this situation is long, stackable bins that extend most of the way from the front to the back of the bed. You can find these at specialty storage stores, and there are options with drawers so that you don't have to pull an entire shallow plastic tote completely out from under the bed every time you want to access that storage.

Key Actions to Take

- [ ] Determine the amount of clearance under your chosen bed height.
- [ ] Choose a front/back plan: easy to access in the front with bulkier storage behind.
- [ ] Discuss shared storage needs with roommate(s) to account for any shared items that may need to be stored under your bed, such as cleaning supplies and paper products.

10

Closet Layouts & Organization

What You'll Take Away

- → An understanding of the most common dorm closet types and how they differ
- → How to design your closet setup based on your top priority: hanging, folded, or shoe storage
- → Organizing ideas for using every inch of vertical and horizontal space
- → Practical tips for lighting, airflow, and maintaining an organized closet all year long

THERE ARE NO STANDARD DORM CLOSETS

Dorm closets come in all shapes and sizes—they vary more than any other part of a dorm room. Some are regular closets with doors like you have at home; others are open nooks with a single rod (or no rod, so you'll need to bring your own); and some are stand-alone wardrobe units, either built-in or mobile. You may have your own closet, or you may share a closet with your roommate.

Most dorm closets come with challenges such as shallow depths, nonideal fixed rod heights, and low or zero lighting. The configuration may not have any space for long-hanging items, or the foot of the bed may be so close to your nook-style closet that you can barely walk between the two.

It is easy to overestimate what will fit in a dorm closet, and overpacking clothes is all too common. Try to focus on what you'll actually wear in the current season, and plan to make seasonal swaps from home if at all possible.

CLOSET LOCATION IN DORM ROOMS

Built-in closets are almost always in one of two places:

1. In the entryway leading to the wider opening of the room where the furniture is
2. In the main part of the room, usually closer to the door than the windows

But there are always exceptions. Some dorm rooms have an entire wall of built-ins along the length of the room, providing closets, desks, and even a sink area.

There are dorms that were built in the 1800s and dorms that are just opening the year you arrive; knowledge and research go a long way toward making an accurate dorm room plan, including a plan for the closet.

Pro Tip: Older dorms may have extra-thick doors, $1^{3}/_{4}$ inches or thicker. Look for adjustable or wider over-the-door hooks for dorm buildings built before 1950. Today's doors are in the $1^{3}/_{8}$-to-$1^{1}/_{4}$-inch range.

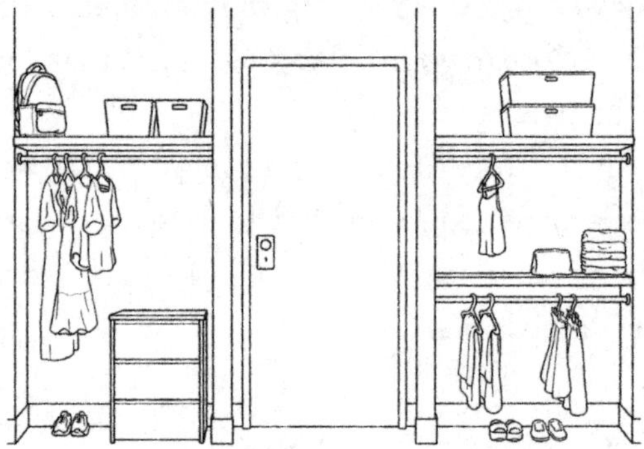

Nook closets on each side of the dorm room entry door—one with a single closet rod (left) and one with double closet rods (right).

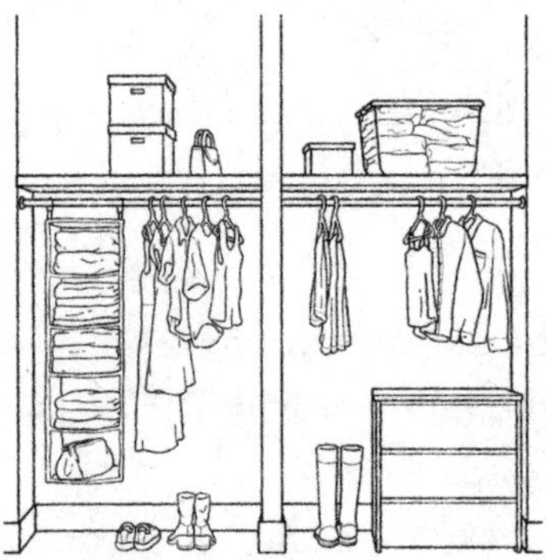

Side-by-side nook closets—one with a fabric hanging shelf (left) and one with the dresser stored in the closet (right).

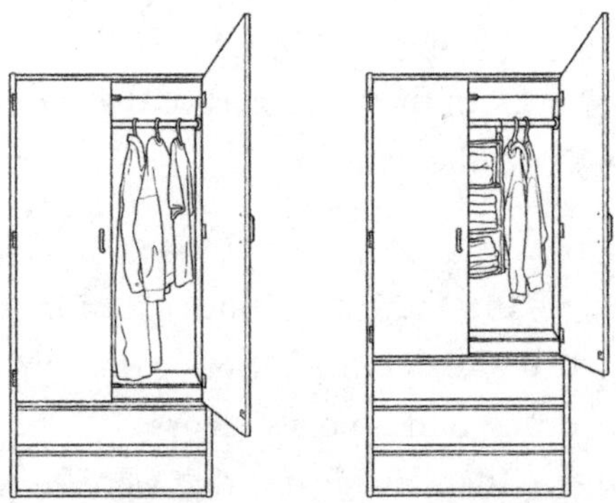

Two wardrobe unit examples—one with a long-hanging space and fewer drawers (left) and one with no room for long-hanging items but with additional drawer space.

CLOSET PLANNING: PRIORITIES DRIVE ORGANIZATION

Consider your storage needs to plan the best closet setup for you. Do you use more hanging space or more drawer space? Do you need a lot of shoe storage? Build your plan around what you need most, and consider flexible solutions if your closet layout is a challenge.

> **Pro Tip:** Don't forget to allocate space in your closet or nearby for a laundry hamper.

1. Maximize Hanging Space
    - Use a rod doubler to create two short-hanging spaces.
    - Choose slim nonslip hangers to save space and prevent slipping.
    - Separate short-hanging and long-hanging sections.
    - For shared closets, mark sides or sections with a strip of painter's tape.
    - Consider folding items and storing them in drawers rather than hanging them.
2. Maximize Folded and Contained Storage
    - Hanging shelves or fabric cubbies work for T-shirts and sweatshirts. Be sure to choose those with thick, reinforced cardboard shelves.
    - Drawer towers, cube organizers, or stackable bins fit beneath short-hanging areas.
    - Utilize additional under-bed storage to create more drawer space.

- Organize a long shelf over a closet rod by using shelf dividers to keep it neat.
- If you have more hanging space than shelf space, use hanging solutions such as hoodie hangers, leggings hangers, and tank top organizers.

3. Maximize Shoe and Accessory Storage
   - Shoe shelves, shoe storage boxes, and hanging shoe cubbies can help in the closet.
   - Under-bed shoe organizers can hold off-season or less frequently worn shoes.
   - Use over-the-door hooks for belts and bags.
   - Consider adhesive hat hooks in the dorm room or hat hangers in the closet.
   - Rotate clothes and shoes by season to avoid overcrowded messes at the bottom of the closet. Off-season shoes can go under the bed.
4. Store More Than Clothes
   - Will you need shelf space for extra linens, towels, or paper products?
   - Hanging storage can work for jewelry, first aid kits, and extra toiletries.
   - Cases of drinks and larger boxes of snacks may need closet floor space.
   - Rolling carts sometimes need to be parked in a closet if there is no room elsewhere.

ONE CLOSET TO SHARE?

If you're sharing one closet with a roommate or roommates, allocate the space equally from the start. Not all closets can be easily split down the middle, so be sure to open with a simple question: "How should we split shelves and hanging space?"

- Divide space evenly (and visually) using stationary dividers or tape.
- Label shelves or drawers to keep things clear.
- If the closet is an open nook, ensure that everyone agrees before adding curtains or other screening.
- Be even more diligent about keeping your part of the closet tidy.

ARE YOU FULLY LOFTING YOUR BED?

If your bed is going up, you've got an opportunity to have hanging storage below! You won't want to hang your clothes out in the open under your bed, but how about purses, baseball caps, or a whole shoe holder full of snacks, school supplies, and odds and ends?

Hang over-the-door organizers from the top of your horizontal bed rail or from the exposed metal springs under the mattress. (Read more about the space under fully lofted beds on page 88.)

LIGHTING, AIRFLOW, AND MAINTENANCE

- Add rechargeable motion-sensing adhesive-mounted LED light strips if the space is dark.
- Skip any scented products; scent sensitivity and allergies may be a concern for your roommate(s) and guests.
- Use charcoal or moisture-absorbing hanging bags to control odor and humidity.
- Do laundry frequently enough so that dirty clothes don't pile up and cause unpleasant odors.

Pro Tip: Schedule a mid-year reset—empty and wipe down dusty spaces, vacuum, and reorganize to match the season.

Implementing a combination of planning, clever storage solutions, and space-saving techniques helps maximize the storage in your dorm closet. Leave space for storing off-season clothes under your bed and declutter and reorganize regularly to make your closet work best for you.

Key Actions to Take

- [ ] **Identify your dorm's closet type and determine measurements and layout.**
- [ ] **Decide what you will store on hangers, folded, or otherwise.**
- [ ] **Pack your hanging items on hangers in bags to simplify setup.**
- [ ] **Discuss shared closet or storage spaces with your roommate as early as possible.**

11

The Multifunctional Desk Area

What You'll Take Away

- How dorm desks and chairs typically vary (sizes, drawers, hutches) and what that means for setup
- A practical plan for one desk to serve four uses: study area, dining table, nightstand, and vanity
- Smart, non-damaging ways to organize, protect surfaces, and manage cables
- Considerations for monitors, mirrors, and storage when a desk hutch is involved

A dorm desk plays more roles than any other piece of furniture in a dorm room. In a single day, it might host a Zoom study session, be used as a hair-drying station before a club event, serve as a recharging zone for multiple battery-drained devices, and provide a spot for eating a messy late-night burrito.

Because the desk is such a busy, multifunctional place, a little planning goes a long way toward helping it perform as needed, when needed. Be sure to understand what the school provides, if the desk can be moved within the room, if there is nearby storage, and what you'll need to do at the desk. Students with a semi-private or private bathroom or a sink in their room can probably scratch using the desk as a vanity off the list.

DORM DESK SIZES AND CONFIGURATIONS

Dorm-provided desks come in a few common configurations. Some are just a simple desktop with four legs. Others may have a single center drawer, while many include stacked drawers on one side.

A minority of schools supply an attached or removable hutch for vertical storage, and some desks even come with built-in lighting.

Desk width can range from 24 to 40 inches or more, with 30 to 36 inches being the most common. If your school provides a three-drawer dresser, it is very likely the same height and depth as the desk. Depending on your room layout and furniture plan, placing the dresser next to the desk creates a long workspace that many find helpful.

DESK PLACEMENT

Depending on your room layout, you may have some flexibility in where to put your desk, or you may have no choice at all. In my son's dorm room, if he and his roommate didn't fully loft their beds, their only option was to put their two desks between their beds and use them as nightstands, too.

A dorm desk next to a three-drawer dorm dresser creates a large desk space.

In many situations, the dorm desk will sit at the foot of the bed, facing either the bed or the wall. In rooms with fully lofted beds, the desks often sit under the beds, leaving more room for mini-kitchen setups.

And in some dorm rooms, the desks are built-in, and you'll need to work around them as you arrange the room. In many built-in situations, you may have the added benefit of built-in shelving or even a permanent bulletin board on the wall above the desk surface.

If you can, determine the locations of the room's outlets ahead of time to gauge the length of your desk surge protector cord and your outlet needs. (More on surge protectors and all the rules around power and electricity in chapter 13.)

DESK HUTCHES

Many students bring their own desk hutch (sometimes called a desk bookcase) if their school does not provide one. Desk hutches are a

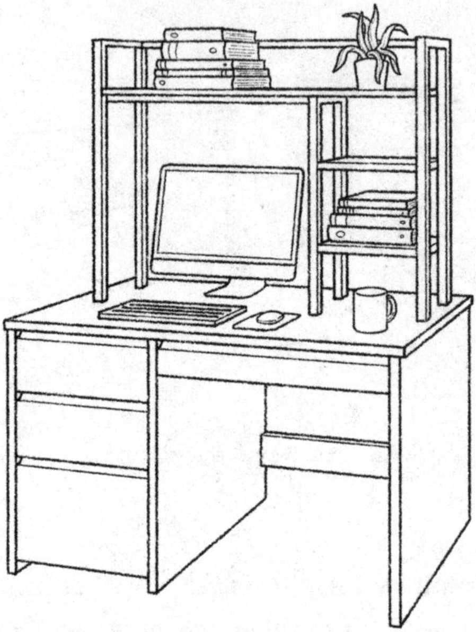

An example of a student-provided desk hutch on a dorm desk.

great way to add vertical storage in a dorm room, especially on the busy desk.

If your desk plan includes a computer monitor and/or a large vanity mirror, please allow enough space for them to fit below the hutch. If those items will not fit below, and must sit in front of the desk hutch, it will be too close to you and also impede on useful space on the desk.

If the clearance is close to fitting your monitor or mirror below but off by under an inch, you can use padded furniture or Velcro strips to help build up your desk hutch height slightly.

In addition to height clearance, be aware that many commercially made desk hutches are for desks over 36 inches wide as most home and office desks are at least this wide. However, dorm desks are sometimes less than 36 inches wide and in some cases, less than

30 inches. It can be difficult to find a desk hutch for these smaller desks, but I have a current list on TheDormGuide.com.

Have a handy person or woodworker in the family? DIY desk hutches are a great idea for custom dimensions and for saving a little money. I've seen a few that also include stick-on puck lights for a bit of extra lighting and ambience.

ONE DESK, FOUR (POTENTIAL) JOBS

Your desk will be busy with up to four potential roles: study area, dining table, nightstand, and vanity. That's a lot to juggle, and it will work best if the desk area is organized and kept clean.

Clean doesn't just mean sanitized. You should also have a plan to protect the desk from spills, makeup, and hair products. A thin acrylic topper cut to size at a home improvement store is a great way to do this (see page 227).

In addition to protecting the surface, be sure to move your electronics out of the way when using the desk for meals or as a vanity station.

The Study Area

Welcome to college, where studying and academics are at a whole new level. While you may do a good bit of studying outside of your room, you'll definitely want a comfortable and well-lit place for doing homework and studying in your dorm room.

Power Supply

I've never seen a dorm room with a good number of electrical outlets. One or two per side of the room (per roommate) is pretty typical. You'll want to bring a surge protector for powering all the items on or used at the desk.

A quality desk lamp for good task lighting and to reduce eye strain is ideal. Try to position it with the least illumination on your roommate's bed.

You'll also want to be able to power your laptop, your phone, and possibly a monitor, keyboard, or other accessories. If the cords start adding up, look to zip ties or adhesive cable clips to help wrangle the cord jungle.

Don't forget to label your electronics, charging blocks, and cables as you're setting them up on your desk.

Internet Connection

It is safe to say that every school has Wi-Fi these days, and it is also safe to say that connection speeds will vary. In schools with a single Wi-Fi network, peak traffic hours and streaming video can slow speeds to a frustrating level.

It is worth checking with your school to see if this is an issue and, if so, whether they also offer wired internet access in the dorm rooms. It might sound antiquated, but connecting an Ethernet cable from your laptop to the wall could make a huge speed difference. It should be under $20 for the Ethernet cable and an adapter for your computer.

Organization and School Supplies

Sometimes visuals help you stay organized. A small dry-erase board for a handwritten to-do list can help reinforce the notes on your phone by keeping them front and center. Keep helpful items such as dry-erase pens, sticky notes, and markers in one container close at hand during study time.

The Dining Table

Unless you're in an apartment-style dorm room, the only table-like surface in your dorm room is your desk. When you have a snack, cook some ramen, or order a pizza, you'll likely end up eating at the desk. Honestly, it is better than sitting on your bed and making a crumby mess.

Keep a container of antibacterial wipes close at hand, and be sure to clean the dishes right after you eat to keep lingering smells out of the room. Your roommate may be trying to study through your fragrant meal!

> **Pro Tip:** When you heat food in the microwave, whether in your room or a common kitchen down the hall, carry it back on a larger plate so that sauces and condensation don't make a trail across your dorm room floor and onto your desk. Leave the food on the plate at your desk to catch any drips or crumbs and make clean-up easier.

The Nightstand

It happens fairly frequently that the only spot for the desk is right next to the bed. This means no room for a separate nightstand, which will save a little of your budget. Still, it also means giving the desk yet another task and carving out space for nightstand necessities like a lamp, clock, phone charging stand, fan, water bottle, book, or journal—whatever you're used to having within an arm's reach.

This is not a big deal, but it is something to plan for in your room. If the other side of the bed is up against the wall, scratch a nightstand off your list. If you want a separate place for bedside objects and there is room, consider a long, narrow bed-height table wedged between the bed and the wall. These are often custom-made and run the length of the bed.

Dorm desk next to the bed and also used as a nightstand.

The Vanity

For many students, the desk doubles as a vanity because it's the only surface with a chair and a place for a well-lit mirror. If you're lucky enough to have a sink and mirror in your dorm room or a private or semi-private bathroom, you may not need to use your desk.

A freestanding makeup mirror with adjustable lighting is popular in dorm rooms and will remain useful in off-campus housing. If you will use a desk hutch, confirm that the mirror at its full standing height will fit under the lowest hutch shelf.

Makeup mirrors aren't very deep, so if you can store the mirror under your desk hutch, it won't take too much space on your desktop; however, storing all the things that come with doing hair and makeup at the desk is a challenge.

If you have desk drawers, this is a good place to store smaller, shorter items. Putting these items into inexpensive drawer organizers makes it easy to pull out one at a time as needed.

You'll also need drawer space for hairbrushes, hair accessories, fragrances, deodorant, body lotion, and any items that are short enough to stand up in a drawer. Use a silicone mat to hold hot hair tools, then unplug them and allow them to cool completely after use before storing. Don't forget to allocate space for cleansers, cotton swabs, cotton balls, and makeup brushes.

If drawers are limited, store frequently used items in a small container on the desk or in the desk hutch. A slim rolling cart or a makeup train case can also keep items close. Keep fragrances capped and store liquids upright; leak-proof pouches are helpful for tiny items that could tip over in a drawer.

Sharing Space

If you have a single sink and mirror in the room, work out a schedule with your roommate(s) for hair and makeup time so you're not competing for space to use hot tools and makeup brushes.

Desk Chairs

Almost all dorm rooms come equipped with a desk chair. Unfortunately, this is almost always an uncomfortable wooden chair. You'll probably spend a good bit of time in this chair—how do you make it comfortable?

Chair pads are widely used, and full chair slipcovers are

sometimes added to make the chair look a little nicer. Honestly, just try out the chair for a week or two, and you can add a cushion later if needed.

Some students bring their own desk chairs. This is fine if you have room to move a chair with all your other dorm essentials, but know that most schools do not allow you to remove any school-provided furniture from your dorm room. You'll need to store the dorm chair under your bed or in another location—and keep in mind that there will not be many places to store a big wooden chair in your dorm room!

CLEANING AND CARE

Pens leak, noodles spill, bronzer crumbles. Keep cleaning supplies, including paper towels, disinfecting wipes, and a small vacuum cleaner, close at hand.

Insects can be an issue in dorm rooms with so many people and so many snacks and crumbs. Clean your desk after meals and vacuum as needed.

If you do use an acrylic desk topper, clean it with mild soap and a microfiber cloth. Avoid cleaning sprays and disinfectants to prevent clouding.

Key Actions to Take

- [ ] **Obtain desk measurements, including those of a hutch, if provided.**
- [ ] **Find out what type of desk chair is provided.**
- [ ] **Measure the height of your computer monitor and makeup mirror if you're taking ones that you already have.**

- [ ] Determine how many outlets are in the room and their approximate location.
- [ ] Ask prior students about their Wi-Fi experience and if wired internet connections are available in the dorm rooms.

12

Dorm Room Mini-Kitchen Setups

What You'll Take Away

- → Rules to verify before deciding on a setup (know if you can bring, must rent, or have to skip a mini fridge and microwave)
- → Options for setting up a dorm room mini kitchen
- → Other popular dorm room appliances to bring (rules permitting)
- → How to plan and share costs with roommates

Are you reading this and thinking, "Hey, what about that unlimited meal plan? Why would a student need a kitchen space?"

I thought that, too, until my two kids lived in dorms.

They frequently cooked (okay, primarily heated food in the microwave) in their dorm rooms.

Students don't always make it to the dining hall for meals, and even if they do, they're hungry again by 10 p.m., when nothing on campus is open. When it is pouring rain or snowing, they may not want to trudge to the dining hall. And dining hall fatigue is *real*, and it can kick in after just a few months.

Setting students up to make simple meals or reheat leftovers goes a long way toward reducing fast-food expenses and late-night delivery orders.

WHAT ABOUT SUITE-STYLE AND APARTMENT-STYLE DORMS?

What is the difference between suite-style and apartment-style rooms? Primarily, it is kitchens.

Suite-style dorm rooms often have private or shared bedrooms, shared bathrooms, and a common area. The common area may just be a small entry hall, or it could be a living room with or without a small space for a "kitchen." There may be some kitchen-like cabinets and counter space, but students typically need to bring or rent their own appliances.

Apartment-style dorm accommodations almost always have a shared living room and kitchen. Don't count on a dishwasher, but the kitchen usually has a fridge, a cooktop, and an oven. If you're really fortunate, you might even have an in-unit washer and dryer. You can confirm these specifics with the housing department before move-in.

Pro Tip: Even if the dorm room or college apartment has a full kitchen, some students choose to bring a mini fridge for their private bedroom, especially if they are a returning student who already has one from previous years. It's a nice way to store your favorite foods and drinks.

APPLIANCES: WHAT IS PERMITTED IN A TYPICAL DORM ROOM?

Let's start with the most significant factor in dorm room mini-kitchen setups: what you are allowed to have in the room and the rules and restrictions for those items.

Mini Fridges

Schools generally have one of the following rules about mini fridges.

- No mini fridges allowed in dorm rooms
- One MicroFridge (combo fridge/microwave) permitted per dorm room, rented through the school or the approved third-party provider
- One personal mini fridge per room, with limitations on cubic feet, wattage, or both
- Very rarely, one personal mini fridge per student, with limitations on cubic feet, wattage, or both

Microwaves

As with mini fridges, microwaves have similar rules and requirements.

- No microwaves allowed in dorm rooms
- Microwaves permitted but limited to 700 or 900 watts or .7 or .9 cubic feet
- One MicroFridge permitted per dorm room, rented through the school or approved third-party provider

(Remember to read chapter 1 for information on what to research and how to research your dorm room.)

Pro Tip: If a MicroFridge is the only allowed appliance, you might be tempted to purchase your own rather than rent year after year. If you are required to live on campus for multiple years, this might make better financial sense, but consider the weight and inconvenience of moving it each year. If you rent, it will be delivered to your room at the beginning of the year and picked up at the end of the year. If you purchase, you'll need to move it in and out each year.

HOW MUCH SPACE DO YOU NEED FOR A MINI FRIDGE?

Keep in mind that most mini fridges, regardless of cubic-foot size, have roughly the same footprint. As the size increases, the height increases. You'll need approximately 2 feet by 2 feet of space for a mini fridge, and a two-door fridge will range in height from about 32 inches to over 50 inches for the larger MicroFridges.

Please confirm size or wattage restrictions with your school.

A side-by-side visual of three popular dorm mini fridges
and two different MicroFridges.

SIMPLE SOLUTIONS AND PLACEMENT OPTIONS

A small kitchen space in a dorm room can range from a simple mini fridge with a microwave on top to a more elaborate mini kitchen complete with storage and room for other appliances. These are a few options for setting up a basic kitchen area.

- **Mini Fridge with Microwave on Top (or MicroFridge):** A simple organizer can live on top of the microwave to hold plates, napkins, and silverware. Any microwave accessories, small appliances, food storage, and unrefrigerated condiments can be kept elsewhere.
- **Mini Fridge with a Basic Fabric Kitchen Organizer over the Top:** The organizer hangs down on each side of the fridge and has pockets similar to those in an over-the-door shoe organizer. Place the microwave on top to keep the organizer in place.
- **Mini Fridge Under a Bed:** There are situations where the only spot for a mini fridge is under a raised bed. In this case, a microwave will have to go elsewhere, along with accessories, food storage, and supplies. Ensure that the fridge has proper

clearance from the vent and is not near any bedding or other fabrics.

EXPANDED MINI-KITCHEN SOLUTIONS

There are several creative ideas for setting up a kitchen space in a dorm room; you'll just need to know your room layout to determine whether one or any of these will work. Each of these explains the space required and the affordable materials you'll need.

While I was not the originator of most of these ideas, I gave them names, found the best products to use, and have helped families with these for years. (You can see specific brand name suggestions and setup guides on TheDormGuide.com.)

The Vertical Dorm Room Kitchen

If you have space for a mini fridge in the room, a vertical kitchen is one of the best ways to utilize 18 to 19 inches of open wall space.

The Ideal Vertical Shelving Unit

The key component of a vertical kitchen is a tall, sturdy shelving unit that fits closely around the mini fridge.

The ideal shelving unit has:

- An 18-by-24-inch footprint and is at least 72 inches tall
- Shelves that are adjustable to any height to accommodate your appliances and storage
- A metal frame (rather than plastic) for sturdiness

Note that the 24-inch side is for the front of the fridge, with the 18-inch side going from the front to the back of the refrigerator. Most mini fridges are a little over 19 inches deep, but you want the front inch to be in front of the rack so the fridge doors can swing freely.

Can You Use Over-the-Toilet Shelving in a Kitchen Setup?

Technically yes, but the shelves are only 9 to 10 inches deep, reducing the storage space by about half, and are not able to hold a microwave or other appliances. In addition, you won't be able to adjust the shelves to meet your needs.

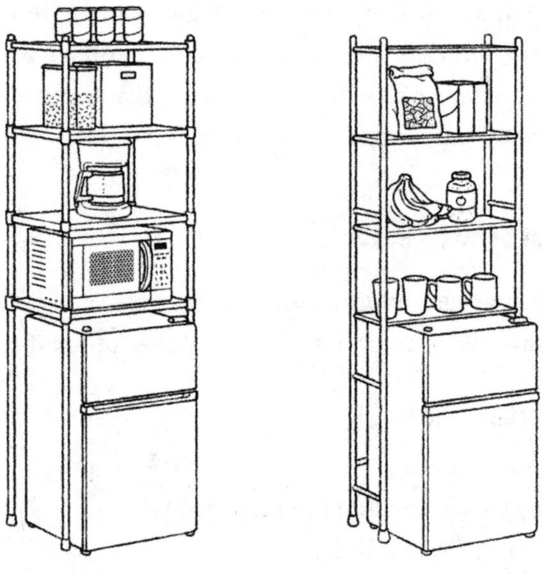

An 18-inch-deep shelving unit (left) provides considerably more storage than a 9- or 10-inch-deep over-toilet shelving unit (right).

Smart Storage Tips

- Use the top shelf for items you won't need frequently. It's a great place for unopened paper towels (and toilet paper if you have a private bath), storage containers that are not in use, and infrequently used appliances.

- Dorm-size microwaves are unlikely to occupy the entire shelf width. Consider an item that would use the space next to it.
- Some appliances open on the top, such as a Keurig coffee maker. Plan your shelving heights to accommodate the opening, leaving room to use the appliance.
- Label storage bins to help keep things organized.
- Consider a step stool for those who cannot reach the upper or top shelf.
- Don't forget a kitchen-size trash can—a standard office- or bathroom-size trash can is not ideal for a dorm room. Choose a narrow stainless steel or plastic trash can with an opening at the narrow end, and place it close to your dorm kitchen.

Reusability After Dorm Life

If you're heading to a school where students tend to move off-campus after one year in the dorm, you will likely still reuse this setup. Why? If they're moving to an apartment or house with several roommates, it's pretty common for students to bring their mini fridge to their private bedroom to keep their own beverages and favorite foods.

Even if they don't need all the food storage, microwave accessories, and small appliances in their room, they'll appreciate that extra vertical storage above—apartment bedrooms are usually small, too!

The Fridge Bridge

A dorm room fridge bridge is pretty simple: It is a mini fridge with an optional microwave above, surrounded by two cube organizers and a long shelf over the top.

A fridge bridge with a 3.1-cubic-foot fridge and a microwave in the middle.

Gather Measurements First

- What is the height of your mini fridge or MicroFridge?
- If you're bringing your own fridge, are you bringing a microwave, too? What is the total height of the two?

You can adjust your fridge bridge for any height—just measure the total height of your fridge and microwave setup.

Be cautious when considering cube organizer substitutes:

- A bookcase on each side or an 11-inch cube organizer on each side will not be deep enough to be a sturdy base for the shelf at the top of the fridge bridge.
- For reference, an 11-inch three-cube organizer is only 36 inches tall and 11.75 inches deep, and a 13-inch three-cube organizer is 43.3 inches tall and 15.3 inches deep.

Where Will You Put the Fridge Bridge in the Dorm Room?

Before we get to the materials needed, let's do a quick check of where the fridge bridge is going in the room.

If you plan to place your fridge bridge between two dorm beds as a dual nightstand (as shown on opposite page), I recommend keeping the combined height of your fridge and microwave under 43 inches to fit a three-cube organizer. This creates the perfect height for a shared nightstand between two captain's-height beds.

If you have about 55 inches of wall space available elsewhere in your room, consider the taller four-cube organizer. With a four-cube organizer, the horizontal shelf will be about 57 inches high, which may be too tall to use as a coffee station or kitchen shelf. That's about chin-height for someone who's 5 foot 5. This can be a good height for a TV stand.

Materials Needed to Create a DIY Dorm Room Fridge Bridge

You need only four things to make a fridge bridge:

- Two 13-inch wood cube organizers (do not use the 11-inch cube organizers, as they are not nearly as sturdy)
- A 15-inch-deep closet shelf cut to length to fit your setup
- A mild adhesive, such as painter's tape, adhesive picture hangers, or rubber bumper pads

The Top Fridge Bridge Shelf

To determine the width needed for the shelf, add the width of the two cube organizers, to the width of the mini fridge, and then add about an inch on each side of the fridge.

Almost all dorm-size fridges, including MicroFridges, are 19 to 20 inches wide. Add two cube organizers, each 16.4 inches wide, and your fridge bridge will be about 53 inches wide. I prefer to cut the shelf to 55 inches, leaving a slight overhang on the sides.

If you are near a home improvement store, you can easily find this "fridge bridge shelf." Look for a closet shelf that is as close as possible to 55 inches long (so probably 60 or 72 inches) and, more important, about 15.5 inches deep. Pick up the shelf and ask a store associate to cut it to 55 inches long. That should be a free service.

Adhesive Option: Rubber Bumper Pads

For added stability, consider placing Velcro strips or small rubber bumper pads on top of the cube organizers to help keep the top shelf in place. Pick these up at your building supply store when you are there to purchase the top shelf. To remove after dorm use, simply use a plastic scraper.

What to Keep on the Fridge Bridge and in the Cube Shelves

This is up to you, depending on where the fridge bridge is located in the room, but some options are:

- Lamps
- Phone charging stand
- Appliances such as a coffee maker, an electric kettle, and a countertop ice maker
- Fan
- Nightstand needs and decor
- Cube inserts or bins
- Food
- Decor

Other Racks and Cabinets

There are metal racks that are more horizontal than vertical. Having significant horizontal space available is unusual, but if you do, consider keeping the kitchen setup lower and using the top for a TV or other helpful eye-level storage.

A mini-fridge cabinet is popular, especially at schools with limited space between the beds. Some local companies offer incredibly expensive custom options, and while some of these custom cabinets can be picked up for less at resale at the end of the school year, they are still pricey.

Due to their popularity, more commercially available cabinets are coming to market. Although they are still far more expensive than a vertical kitchen or a fridge bridge, if you decide to go this route, please ensure that the cabinet is open at the back to allow proper ventilation for the mini fridge and microwave.

> **Pro Tip:** Never put a mini fridge or a microwave inside an enclosed cabinet. You have probably seen beverage fridges built into cabinetry in homes, but those fridges are far more expensive front-vented models.

SAFETY AND CLEANING

Along with closely following all dorm rules related to appliances, please adhere to the following safety guidelines:

- Never plug a mini fridge or microwave into an extension cord. Most dorms do not allow extension cords anyway, but for safety, refrain from using them even if they are allowed.

- If you must plug a mini fridge into a surge protector, never daisy-chain (plug multiple strips into one another) surge protectors.
- Always ensure that there is proper airflow behind the fridge and microwave. The refrigerator needs to vent out of the back, so ensure that it has enough space. Never put a mini fridge in a closed cabinet.

In dorm kitchen areas and during food preparation, cleaning is important not only for health reasons but also to prevent insects from helping themselves to food and crumbs.

- If you have only a shallow bathroom sink for washing dishes and cleaning appliance parts, use a deep plastic bin and mild detergent to make cleanup easier and more thorough.
- Do not bring appliances that are hard to clean or won't be adequately cleaned during the year.
- You will almost certainly need to empty your mini fridge before winter break, so plan to use up the refrigerated contents and follow the manufacturer's instructions to properly defrost it before break.

SHARING KITCHENS AND SETUP COSTS WITH ROOMMATES

I recommend dividing the items to buy into roughly equal portions rather than splitting the cost between roommates without a plan for who gets to take which items at the end of the school year. More information on planning with roommates can be found on page 76.

Key Actions to Take

- ☐ Check your specific dorm rules regarding appliances and electrical items.
- ☐ Determine the room layout and research how prior residents have set up mini kitchens in your specific dorm room layout.
- ☐ If you are creating a fridge bridge, formulate a list of equipment needed before visiting a home improvement store.
- ☐ Connect with your roommate to determine if they want to use the kitchen space and if so, how to split the cost.

13

Power, Lighting & Tech

What You'll Take Away

- An expert-level understanding of all things surge protectors
- Where to consider placing your own task and ambient lighting
- Electronics and tech to bring or leave at home
- Important considerations and potential cost savings on a laptop for college

If there is one thing that's consistent about electrical items and related rules for dorm rooms, it is the full-fledged inconsistency across college campuses. This chapter walks you through rules to look out for, safety requirements and recommendations, and answers to the frequently asked questions about technology, lighting, and safely powering a dorm room. As with all things, and especially with electrical devices, research the rules for the dorm room carefully.

A NOTE ABOUT UL SAFETY

One requirement that is becoming more widespread is that all electronics must be UL Listed. The "UL safety mark" means a product has been certified to meet scientific safety, quality, or security standards. Look for UL safety marks on product packaging, on the product itself, or in the product details section when shopping online.

It isn't always easy to find UL Listed certified items that you plan to bring. But "ETL Listed" is another American safety testing company that follows UL standards, and many schools will accept both ETL Listed and UL Listed products. You may not find this information on the housing website, so please confirm this with Housing before purchasing electrical products.

Is all this checking really necessary? It definitely is: The RAs will often check at move-in and likely at other times during the school year.

POWERING THE DORM ROOM

Power rules vary by school. Most allow specific surge-protected power strips but ban extension cords or daisy-chaining. Surge-protected strips are designed to plug directly into a wall outlet only.

Surge Protector Strips

In my years of helping families plan for college life, I've learned of a new rule for surge protectors at least once per year. The following are rules, restrictions, or maximums/minimums that I've encountered over time:

- Restrictions on the number of surge protectors per student
- Maximum cord length
- Maximum number of receptacles permitted on the surge protector
- Minimum number of joules (how much of a surge it can handle)
- Whether the surge protector has two-prong or three-prong outlets
- Certification such as UL or ETL Listed
- Whether there's an on/off switch on the surge protector

Additionally, although this is not typically required, I prefer surge protectors with flat plugs because most outlets are inconveniently located behind furniture. Also, ensure that the surge protector accepts three-prong plugs where allowed.

Most students also want USB ports in their surge protectors, but finding them is hard, along with meeting the other school rules and requirements.

Wall-mounted surge protectors, which are cordless and provide extra outlets directly at the original outlet, are typically less helpful. Since most outlets are behind furniture, using a surge-protected power strip will be easier than dealing with several wall outlets, especially since extension cords are rarely permitted.

You'll want at least two long surge protectors for your side of the room, if permitted.

Safety Tip: Never plug mini fridges into an extension cord (if extension cords are allowed). They should be plugged into a wall outlet, preferably, or into a surge-protected power strip.

LIGHTING FOR DORM ROOMS

Most dorm rooms come equipped with one especially bright fluorescent ceiling light. Powered by the on/off switch by the door only, it is an all-or-nothing in your dorm room—harsh bright light or complete darkness. If your roommate comes in at 3 a.m. and turns on the light, it will be a rude awakening.

A few lamps in the room are helpful for late-night study sessions, late-returning roommates, and early risers.

Desk Lamps

Consider a desk lamp not only for late-night focused light but also to improve eye strain while reading or working at the desk. Some models come with charging pads or ports, as well as color and/or brightness selection options.

Nightstand Lamps

If you have a nightstand, a lamp is always a nice addition, providing both reading light and ambience in the room. Roommates often choose identical lamps for room symmetry. If a dorm room is designed with the desk positioned in between the dorm beds, a desk lamp can double as a nightstand lamp.

Reading Lights

For those with fully lofted beds or no space for a nightstand, a reading light that clips to the bed or attaches directly to a book helps you read or study in bed.

Floor Lamps

Depending on the room setup, a floor lamp may be a perfect solution. If table space is limited, a floor lamp requires little floor space and provides ambient lighting for the room.

String and Strip Lights

These are sometimes permitted, and if so, they typically come with rules limiting the type and method of hanging. Please check your specific dorm rules before using strip or string lights.

WATCHING SHOWS AND SPORTS: TVS AND ACCESSORIES

Yes, many college students watch streaming content on their phones, but some prefer to view shows and sports on larger screens. TVs are often brought to suite-style dorm rooms with a common living area.

Available Services

Check with your school to determine whether cable TV services are provided or available, and if so, whether you'll need any equipment, such as a coaxial cable, to connect to them. With the increasing popularity of streaming services and smart TVs, many schools are phasing out traditional cable offerings, although they may still be available in the building's common areas.

My son's school offers two Wi-Fi networks: one for school-related work and one for streaming and gaming. Before investing in a TV or other devices, ensure that your school has sufficient bandwidth to support thousands of students streaming daily.

Smart TVs and Streaming Sticks

Smart TVs are equipped with streaming apps, allowing viewers to stream directly on their TVs, but you don't need a new smart TV to stream.

Streaming sticks, such as Roku or Fire versions, plug into any TV via an HDMI port, allowing you to stream content directly to your TV. Most streaming sticks come with a remote control, allowing you to switch between services and shows easily.

Where to Put a TV in a Dorm Room?

This will depend on your layout and furniture configuration, but in all cases, you can't mount it on the wall. If you're fully lofting beds, a lounge area below may include a TV under one bed and a sitting area under the other. For regular-height bed setups, popular options include placing a TV on a dresser, on the top of a desk hutch, or on a mobile TV cart.

> **Safety Tip:** If placing a TV on a dresser or desk hutch, use Velcro strips to keep the TV base in place and the TV from accidentally being knocked off the surface.

Mini Projectors

An alternative to a TV is a mini projector, which is affordable, compact, and easy to move from one room to another, to a common area in the dorm building, or to other locations. Some projectors come with a large projection screen, or you can simply project onto a blank wall and invite friends to watch a show or a big game.

To project streamed content, you'll need to connect a streaming stick or laptop, since most streaming services' rights management doesn't allow shared streaming from phones.

LAPTOPS AND ACCESSORIES

Do you need a laptop for college? Can you just use a tablet with a keyboard to take notes and write papers?

I won't provide suggestions for the best laptops (or tablet alternatives) for college because, as with dorm layouts and rules, each school and department within the school may have specific requirements for each major.

Once you have a college decision, check the school's department website for technology requirements. If you are unable to find the laptop requirements there, check with the school bookstore; they often have a list of requirements by major. Look for requirements around operating system (Windows or Mac), processor speed, memory (RAM), and storage.

Please do not look up the requirements of one school's major department and assume your school will be the same. If an older sibling was a nursing major at one school, please do not assume that a younger nursing major sibling at a different school will need the same configuration.

Laptop Shopping for College

Start with your school bookstore. Not only should the staff there be able to inform you of the requirements by major, but the store may also offer special education pricing, as well as warranty and repair plans.

Be sure to also check manufacturer websites, as most offer education pricing or promotions. Costco and Best Buy sometimes have even better pricing, so it's always worth a quick check once you've decided on the model that will be best for your major at your school.

Computer Accessories

Common accessories for college include:

- External monitor—ensure that the monitor fits below any desk hutch (see page 137 for more on desk configurations)
- Ethernet cable and adapter—if Wi-Fi is rumored to be slow at the school, and wired internet is available in dorm rooms
- External hard drive or cloud storage for backup

Printers are uncommon in dorm rooms, although some students prefer to have their own. Most schools offer printing services in the library and at other campus locations for a small fee. Considering the cost of purchasing your own printer plus toner cartridges, the small fees are reasonable. If you bring a printer, make sure you have a cable to connect it directly to your laptop or other device; you will almost certainly not be able to connect a Wi-Fi-enabled printer to campus Wi-Fi for security reasons.

OTHER HELPFUL COLLEGE TECH

Tablets

Tablets such as iPads, along with stylus pens/pencils, are great for note-taking. Helpful note-taking apps are also available, as are screen protectors that make writing on the screen feel like writing on paper.

Earbuds and Headphones

Earbuds are so popular that having one white earbud in while walking around campus feels almost like a fashion statement. Noise-canceling headphones are helpful for focused studying as well as muting outside noise during airplane or train travel.

Tracking Devices

Tracking tags or tiles can help you keep up with your important items and valuables. Place one in your backpack, on your bike, in your gym bag, or even hidden in your car.

Phone Chargers and Accessories

Why are charging blocks and charging cords always missing? Be sure to label those before arriving on campus, and consider a charging station in the dorm room so phones, headphones, and watches can always be charged.

Portable charging blocks are essential for safety and convenience. Phones are in constant use at college, and students need to keep them charged for day-to-day use and emergencies.

TECH TO CONSIDER LEAVING AT HOME

Smart Devices

Phones and laptops have built-in security features that enable easy identification and authentication by the university's network. You log in with your student credentials, and the IT system knows it's you.

Smart devices, such as smart speakers, smart lights, and smart appliances, lack login capabilities, meaning they can't enter a username and password or access the university's login process. They're designed to connect through a Wi-Fi network, which usually doesn't meet campus security requirements.

All schools prioritize maintaining the security of their networks. Smart devices are often less secure and can serve as entry points for hackers or network attacks; therefore, most campuses simply don't allow them on the network.

Occasionally, I'm asked if bringing your own network router is a good idea, but most schools prohibit external routers for these same security reasons.

Gaming Consoles

Every student is different, but for many students, it is a good idea to leave distractions, including gaming devices, at home, at least for the first semester. If a student struggles with self-regulation at home, it will likely be even more challenging at school.

However, some students find balance and use gaming for social purposes, playing online with friends who are far away. Some colleges also have gaming clubs and competitive e-sports teams.

As with almost all things in college, everything in moderation.

Alarm Clocks

It is fine to bring a clock for the dorm room, but if roommates are involved, I recommend leaving loud alarm clocks at home. Use your phone or smartwatch to wake you more quietly, hopefully without disturbing others in the room.

And speaking of being considerate, if you are a chronic alarm snoozer, now is a good time to break that habit. I receive numerous complaints every year from frustrated students whose roommates hit snooze for an hour or two before finally getting out of bed. Meanwhile, the frustrated roommate has been awake since the alarm first went off!

Key Actions to Take

- ☐ **Confirm campus rules for power strips, extension cords, lighting, and smart devices before shopping.**
- ☐ **Discuss lighting ideas with roommates before shopping.**
- ☐ **Wait for a final college decision before buying a laptop for college to ensure that it meets the department's tech requirements.**
- ☐ **Make sure the student has a tech backup plan, either through an external hard drive or cloud-based storage. Include the laptop, tablet, and phone in this plan.**

14

Furniture for Dorm Rooms

What You'll Take Away

- Which dorm furniture is provided by most colleges
- Additional furniture to consider if space and rules permit
- Options for fully lofted bed layouts
- Which furniture to avoid entirely
- How to plan now for reusability and repurposing

Most dorm rooms come equipped with the same set of basics: a bed (often a twin XL or larger), a mattress, a desk and desk chair, a dresser, and a wardrobe unit if there is no permanent closet in the room. These items are typically made of solid wood but sometimes incorporate metal frames.

They are designed to last through years of student use, and have often seen better days.

Some schools permit moving, stacking, or bunking furniture, while others have specific rules about what must remain as-is. Before planning any adjustments, check your housing website to see what the assigned dorm building allows.

Even with these basics, students often need a few pieces to make the space more comfortable or to add storage. A nightstand, multipurpose ottoman, or small lounge chair all come in handy if space permits. The key is to do your research in advance and always keep scale and moving effort in mind.

As always, please check with your school first regarding furniture.

- Some schools prohibit all outside furniture. Check their definition of furniture, as that could mean something as simple as a small cube organizer.
- Some have restrictions on furniture types, limiting them by size, weight, or materials.
- Some say no to furniture with charging ports.
- Some strictly require flame-resistant or flame-retardant materials.
- Most require that you keep all dorm-provided furniture in the room.

Pro Tip: Before move-in, look up your dorm's floor plan and furniture specifications and use painter's tape at home to mock up the size of the room. The garage is a great place to do this, and it is a quick way to visualize what will actually fit and what won't.

NIGHTSTANDS

Most dorm rooms don't come with nightstands, and when they do, the nightstands are typically quite small and only 24 to 28 inches tall, which will feel very short next to a raised bed. If you have the space, adding a nightstand can be a great way to increase storage and provide a bedside surface for essentials like a lamp, phone charger, water bottle, and even a book.

The sleep surface of dorm beds, raised to the top height of an adjustable bed (captain's height), sits at 37 to 41 inches.

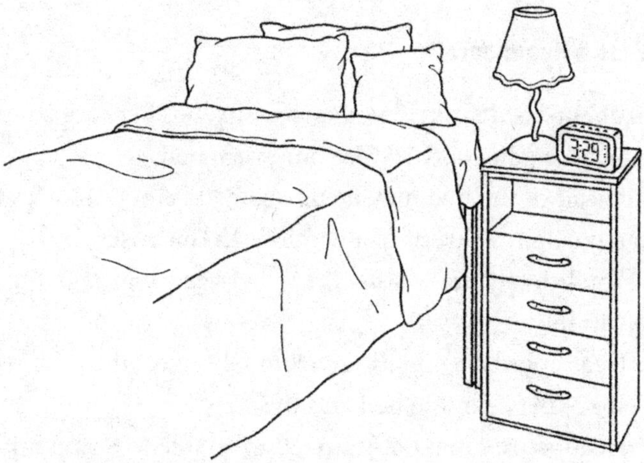

A 40-inch-tall nightstand next to a raised (captain's-height) dorm bed. Raised-height (captain's-height) bed: 30 inches' clearance to the floor (on average). Dorm mattress: 5 to 8 inches thick. Mattress topper: 2 to 3 inches thick. Top layer: 37 to 41 inches off the floor.

Ensure that the following things are allowed:

- Fabric Drawers: Many students opt for a metal-frame nightstand with fabric drawers because these units weigh considerably less than their wood counterparts.

- Charging Ports: Built-in outlets, USB ports, and small LED lights are also popular on taller nightstands.
- Furniture in Front of Windows or Air Vents: This is often the location for a nightstand.

HEADBOARDS

Dorm beds typically don't have a headboard or footboard unless you lower the horizontal spring deck enough that a good part of the bed frame is above the mattress.

Do You *Need* a Headboard?

No, a headboard is definitely not a necessity, but here are a few reasons to consider a headboard for your dorm bed.

1. The head of the bed may be up against a cinder block wall or even partially in front of a window. In this case:
   - You'll likely want something between you and the wall/window.
   - Headboards keep pillows from falling off the end into the space between the bed and the wall.
   - Headboards make it more comfortable to sit up and lean back in bed.
2. The head of the bed may be "floating" in the room with nothing behind it. This is more common with fully lofted beds and bunk beds. In this case:
   - Headboards help keep pillows from falling to the floor while you sleep.
   - Headboards give you the capability to sit up and/or lean back in bed.
3. In a tiny space with many limitations on decor and comfort, a

headboard is a great way to add some style as well as comfort to your dorm room.

Headboard Types, Sizes, and Styles

Headboard Pillows and Cushions

If the bed is directly up against a wall, a headboard pillow or even a dog bed can provide cushioning for sitting up in bed and leaning back against the wall.

Headboard with Legs

If the bed is floating in the room, a headboard with legs is the only option. This is the same type of headboard you might buy for a bed at home. The legs have slots for connecting a standard bed frame, but dorm beds do not have these slots or a way to attach a headboard.

So how do you attach a dorm headboard with legs to a dorm bed? Use several 18- to 24-inch heavy-duty zip ties to attach each headboard leg to the bed frame. You'll need two people—one to hold the headboard in the desired position and one to attach the zip ties. Place a zip tie around the headboard leg and bed-frame leg right above each horizontal bed-frame slat on both sides, and pull them as tightly as possible. Snip off excess zip tie length.

IMPORTANT: The headboard legs will not touch the floor, whether you are attaching the headboard to a regular-height bed or a fully lofted bed, and that is okay!

To add stability, especially for a bed without a wall directly behind, pay attention to how the legs are attached to the headboard—they are likely height-adjustable. Exposing more of the leg below the headboard provides more opportunities to attach zip ties vertically down the leg.

At the end of the school year, use a pair of scissors or snippers to cut the zip ties. Have someone hold the headboard while the ties are being removed to prevent it from falling to the floor.

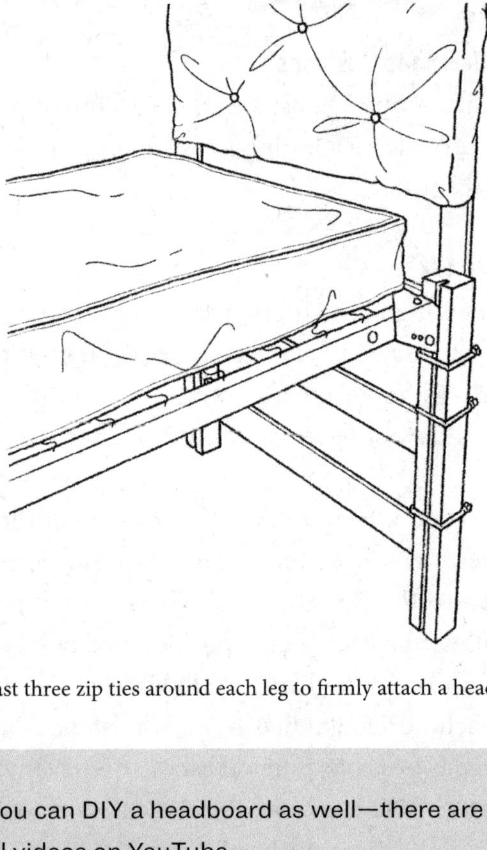

Use at least three zip ties around each leg to firmly attach a headboard.

Pro Tip: You can DIY a headboard as well—there are many instructional videos on YouTube.

What Size Headboard to Use?

Twin XL beds are the same width as the regular-length versions of the bed, so there are no twin XL or full XL headboards. XL beds are

5 inches longer than their standard counterparts, but their width remains the same.

- Twin or twin XL dorm bed = twin headboard (38 to 40 inches wide)
- Full or full XL dorm bed = full headboard (54 inches wide)
- Queen bed = queen headboard (60 inches wide)

OTTOMANS

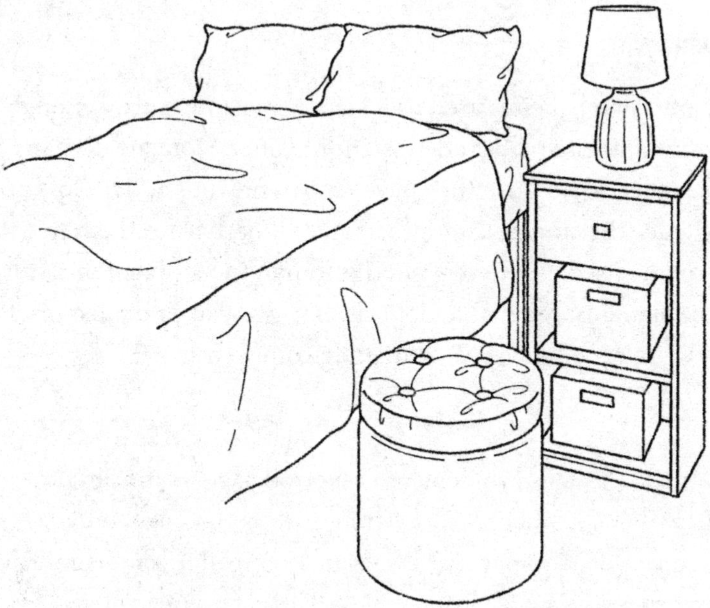

An ottoman next to a raised (captain's-height) dorm bed.

Ottomans are a popular item for dorm rooms due to their multipurpose utility. These are the many ways an ottoman may be useful in a dorm room:

- As a step up to a raised bed
- As extra seating for visitors

- As a portable seat to take to hall gatherings and common areas
- As a footstool when you're sitting in your desk chair
- As a bit of extra (hidden) storage if using a storage ottoman

The good news is that if it survives freshman year in a dorm, it will be reusable in future years, whether you're living in a dorm or in off-campus housing.

Sturdiness

If the ottoman is being used as a step, it must be sturdy enough to withstand the force of a student standing on it. Storage ottomans are not designed to do this! They have removable tops and hollow middles (hence the storage), and this makes it harder for them to withstand being used as a step. A solid ottoman (no storage) or a sturdy step stool are more reliable options, but you can find a list of ottomans we've tested on TheDormGuide.com website.

> **Safety Tip:** Many injuries are reported each year from ottomans tipping when used as steps. Please use caution when stepping on ottomans and always step in the center rather than near an edge.

Size

Height: A typical stair riser is 8 inches, and most students need the equivalent of two steps to reach a 40-inch-high surface. Therefore, ottomans that are 15 to 18 inches tall are best.

Length: If you're using an ottoman for storage, you may be tempted to buy a long one, but dorm room space is tight, and you may not want to go larger than a square size.

Material

The ottoman material is up to you and your decor preferences, but keep practicality in mind if this ottoman will be used as a step. If your student will diligently take off their shoes before stepping on it, a light-colored sherpa or bouclé material will be okay. For those less likely to be delicate, an easy-to-clean faux leather material may be a better option.

Features

Feet: Ottomans with feet can present a tipping hazard, so I would avoid them. The feet can likely be left off during assembly if you already have your heart set on a particular model that has them.

Portable: A foldable ottoman seems like a good idea, allowing you to easily move it out of the way or take it with you; however, foldable ottomans simply can't withstand regular use as a step.

CHAIRS

I prefer a sturdy yet inexpensive folding camp chair for college. It serves as guest seating in a dorm room, can be easily transported for hanging out in the quad or spending a day at the lake, and is easy to store when not in use.

If you have a slightly larger dorm room or a spare corner in a single room, consider adding a more comfortable lounge chair.

Folding butterfly or saucer chairs are popular, as are more elaborate cushioned chairs with small footstools.

As mentioned, some students prefer to bring their own desk chair and store the less comfortable dorm-provided chair elsewhere in their room.

FUTONS

Although it's rare without fully lofting the bed, some traditional double dorm rooms have space for a futon couch or loveseat. Futons are popular as they are lighter than a standard couch, and the back can be lowered to create a flat sleeping area for overnight guests.

Futons are typically 65 to 72 inches long, which makes them a good size to fit below a fully lofted 80-inch-long twin XL dorm bed. Some futon frames have cup holders, small tables in the center, or charging ports. A long rectangular storage ottoman works well in front of a futon, since you should not need to stand on this ottoman.

BOOKSHELVES AND CUBE ORGANIZERS

When floor space is limited, make use of vertical space where possible. Tall cube towers or narrow bookcases create extra space for books, decor, and supplies. Just confirm that your school allows freestanding shelving—some schools prohibit furniture taller than a certain height for safety reasons.

Furniture Discussed in Other Chapters

The below items are discussed in more detail on the following pages:

Desk hutches—page 137

Desk chairs—page 143

Kitchen setups—page 146

Under-bed drawers, dressers, and storage solutions—page 114

OTHER FURNITURE CONSIDERATIONS

Space planning is crucial, as is following all dorm rules regarding outside furniture, but there are additional considerations that I urge you to consider.

Reuse and Repurpose

Waste is a big issue with items brought to dorm rooms. I am on a mission to reduce the number of dumpsters filled with perfectly usable items that are discarded on move-out day due to poor planning.

For *everything* you bring into a dorm room—not just furniture—please consider what will happen to it at the end of the school year. Broken items or those that are filthy beyond cleaning should be discarded; everything else requires a plan. Everything should either be returned home, sold, donated, or stored in a local storage unit.

Before you make dorm purchases, please consider what can be reused in subsequent years, whether the plan is to live on campus or move off-campus.

Durability and Cleanability

Dorm life is tough on furniture, bedding, and rugs. Prioritize sturdy, wipeable surfaces and washable fabrics where possible. Lightweight plastic, metal, or composite wood pieces tend to hold up better than delicate finishes. Focus on affordable, reusable items to ideally last throughout college, and avoid any expensive upholstered items with hard-to-clean fabric.

Furniture to Skip

It's easy to get swept up in decorating ideas, but there are a few items that should be avoided completely:

- **BULKY SOFAS AND PULL-OUT COUCHES:** They are heavy, hard to move, may not fit in the dorm's elevator or through the dorm room door, or fit easily in the dorm room.
- **LARGE RECLINERS:** In addition to being heavy to move, they likely won't fit through the dorm room door.
- **HEAVY WOODEN FURNITURE:** Likely too bulky, difficult to move, and often against housing rules.
- **DESKS:** I have seen students try to bring a standing desk (with a walking pad!) to a dorm room. These are impractical in a small space. You can add an adjustable lap desk to a desk to create a temporary standing desk.
- **GLASS OR MIRRORED PIECES:** Full-length over-the-door mirrors and makeup mirrors are okay but will need to be handled carefully. Adding any other glass or mirrored furniture to a dorm room is very risky.

Key Actions to Take

- ☐ Review your dorm's furniture list and floor plan before purchasing any add-ons.
- ☐ Prioritize lightweight, multiuse furniture that can be easily moved or stored.
- ☐ Coordinate with your roommate to avoid duplicates.
- ☐ Consider adding smaller items, such as bedside trays, lap desks, or rolling carts, for extra flexibility.
- ☐ Plan for move-in day adjustments—they are almost inevitable.

15

Everything to Know About Dorm Bathrooms

What You'll Take Away

- **The two types of bathrooms that are typically found in dorm buildings**
- **What to pack (and what not to pack) for each type of bathroom**
- **How to keep personal items clean, organized, dry, and mildew-free**
- **The best types of towels for college**

Planning what you'll need to bring for your dorm room bathroom may not sound like the most exciting part of going to college, but it is important! Residence halls may have communal bathrooms or private bathrooms, and what to bring will be closely tied to the bathroom location and whom it is shared with.

A quick definition of bathroom types so that we're on the same page:

COMMUNAL BATHROOM: A residence hall bathroom shared by multiple residents. These bathrooms typically consist of multiple shower and toilet stalls, as well as multiple sinks, often in an industrial-style design with mirrors above. Students have no storage space in these bathrooms, so they carry their toiletries and personal items back and forth to their dorm rooms.

PRIVATE BATHROOM: Residence hall bathrooms that are attached to dorm rooms. These are not big communal bathrooms—they may be any of the following:

- A private bathroom in a single room
- A private bathroom shared by more than one dorm room
- A private or shared bathroom in a suite-style or apartment-style dorm room

I've combined these into one category since the preparation and packing needs are the same.

It may seem like a new thing, but private and semi-private dorm bathrooms have actually been around for quite some time. My son lived in a dorm built in 1934 where the residents shared one bathroom for every two rooms. In fact, his entire school only has private or semi-private bathrooms.

This chapter begins with separate sections specific to planning for each of these bathroom styles, followed by information relevant to either situation.

COMMUNAL BATHROOMS

Usually at the end of the hall, but sometimes in the middle, communal baths are similar to locker room bathrooms with a series of shower stalls, toilet stalls, and an open area with sinks and mirrors above each sink.

The good news is that students are not responsible for cleaning these bathrooms, and they are usually cleaned daily, but that doesn't always mean they are cleaned well or stay clean throughout the day.

Communal Bathroom Storage

Communal bathrooms do not offer storage for personal items. Students must bring their personal items with them.

Most students will carry a shower caddy with toiletries and other shower essentials. The area inside or outside the shower should have a hook or shelf to hang or place the caddy on, but if not, bring an S-hook or a carabiner to hang it from the shower curtain rod or showerhead. This is a good topic to research in a parent Facebook group for the school or a student-focused Instagram page.

For trips to the bathroom to brush your teeth or wash your face, a smaller container will be easier and hopefully have a place to hang near the sink. Be sure to bring a toothbrush case or cover to keep the toothbrush as clean as possible.

What to Wear to the Communal Bathroom

Bathrobes, towel wraps, towels, boxer shorts—there really isn't one answer. I've heard from parents moving their sons into the freshman dorm that they had to look away a few times. Just be prepared for anything as you enter the dorm hallways!

Let's talk about shoes, though. Shower shoes are a *must* for communal bathrooms. Some people prefer styles with weep holes in the footbeds to allow water to drain through, but others dislike them because they fear the water may seep up through them. Personal choice!

If slippers are preferred for non-shower trips to the bathroom, be sure they have indoor/outdoor soles. The thicker the sole, the better—the slippers may even find themselves going to class or out for a quick food pickup. I suggest not spending a ton on slippers for dorm life—they may not survive a full semester, let alone a full school year!

Shower Caddies

There are two types of shower caddies—plastic and mesh—and each has pros and cons.

Plastic-molded shower caddies are easy to carry and come in various sizes to meet your toiletry storage needs. They are easy to clean with soap and water or disinfecting wipes. They are harder to hang on a hook or shower rod, but using an S-hook can help.

Mesh shower caddies are lighter and hold a lot. They are easier to hang and balance from a hook, but they are hard to clean and can get mildewy fairly easily. Some are made to be machine-washable, which is very helpful.

Showerheads and Water Quality

Common complaints each year include low water pressure and poor water quality. Reports of acne and changes to hair are frequent, leaving many wondering whether they can change the showerheads in these communal bathrooms.

Obviously, this should not be done without permission. I have heard of situations where the residents on the hall appealed to their RA and got approval to change out the showerheads for the school year.

A simple solution is to try a clarifying shampoo, which can help offset hard water.

After the Shower—Getting Ready

Rather than bringing all their hair and makeup supplies to a busy, steamy communal bathroom, most students set up a vanity space at their desk.

Be sure to follow the dorm rules regarding electrical appliances, and always use a silicone or other heat mat to protect the desk from hot hair tools.

For more details on setting up a vanity space at the desk, see page 142.

Pro Tip: You come back from the shower with a wet shower caddy, wet shower shoes, and a wet towel and washcloth, and walk into your 75-to-100-square-foot dorm room—where are you going to put all these things to dry?

I love a boot tray for this purpose; you can pick one up from a big-box retailer for about $5. Boot trays are a great place to store wet umbrellas, backpacks, and shoes, too. A dish-drying tray works, too, and is a little smaller. You will need to allocate some space in your room for the tray—ideally, by the door, but that is not possible with some dorm room layouts. See the section regarding towels beginning on page 192.

PRIVATE AND SHARED BATHROOMS

This category includes a private bathroom in a single room, a shared bathroom in a single room, a bathroom shared by more than one dorm room, and a private or shared bathroom in a suite- or apartment-style room.

If multiple roommates will share a bathroom, decide in advance who will bring which items. Some dorm room layouts may include a sink in the room, and only the shower and toilet in the shared space.

Where possible, consider a night-light in the bathroom to avoid harsh overhead light late at night and early in the morning, especially if the bathroom opens directly into a sleeping area.

Shower Setup

Unless the shower has a glass enclosure, you'll need the following:

- Shower curtain
- Shower curtain liner—bring a couple
- Shower curtain rings

Either way, you'll also need a bath mat (bring several) and maybe some in-shower storage.

Shower Curtain—Size Matters

Standard shower curtains for bathtub-length showers are typically 72-by-72 inches.

If your bathroom has a stall shower, please check with your school for the exact measurements. However, you will likely need a 36-by-72-inch shower curtain. Avoid using a regular-size curtain in stall-width showers, as it will struggle to dry due to the extra material always bunched up—this could create an environment for mold and mildew to form.

Bath Mats

Many students are inclined to choose a big, fluffy bath rug as part of their bathroom decor, but please choose a practical one for shared bathrooms!

With multiple students showering every day, a thick bath rug will be constantly wet. Bath rugs, although machine-washable, tend to deteriorate over time, particularly when laundered in commercial campus laundry machines.

I recommend using towel-type bath mats, similar to those found in hotels, and having multiple available. These dry faster and are easier to wash and dry in campus laundry rooms. They are affordable and easy to swap out—have each roommate bring a couple so there is always a dry one available.

In-Shower Storage

Stall showers rarely have ledges or niches to store shower supplies, and many bathroom-width showers do not either.

Options for in-shower storage include:

- Over-the-showerhead caddies
- Vertical storage shelf tension rod shelving from the ceiling to the shower floor or ledge
- Adhesive shower shelves

Sink Space

Private bathroom sink areas vary widely. Some dorm rooms will have a sink, which is a nice amenity. Sinks in the shared bathroom can range from a single industrial-style sink with no counter space to a long counter with multiple sinks and ample counter space.

You'll definitely want to find out the details before planning for bathroom storage.

Often, the sinks do not have cabinets below, leaving open space beneath the counter. Rolling three-drawer carts are a great solution in this situation. There may be room for each student to have their own, or only enough room for all of the students to share one. Drawer carts are preferred over open utility carts to protect the contents from bathroom germs and droplets.

After the Shower—Getting Ready

If the sink is in your dorm room, you can use that sink and mirror space as the getting-ready/vanity area.

With a sink in a shared bathroom, you'll probably need to limit time in the bathroom and get ready in the dorm room using the desk as a vanity, as described on page 142.

Additional Bathroom Storage

For bathrooms with limited under-sink storage space, over-the-toilet shelving units can be helpful. I recommend using closed containers on the shelves due to the toilet's proximity and the potential for airborne droplets.

In addition to toiletries, you'll need to plan for storage for toilet paper and cleaning supplies.

Cleaning and Disinfecting

Some schools clean private bathrooms, but these are the exception! In most cases, the students will need to clean showers, toilets, sinks, and floors. These are good life skills that should be learned well before leaving for college.

Develop a weekly roommate cleaning plan and timeline, and hold each other accountable for cleaning on your assigned days. Include a toilet paper purchasing schedule that rotates whose turn it is to buy the next pack.

TOWELS

If your student is heading to a dorm or even a college apartment, they are going to have to forgo super thick, super fluffy, super absorbent towels for a few years.

Regardless of the bathroom situation, it is essential to choose quick-dry towels for dorm life. Dorms are typically damp and humid, and they lack proper (or any) ventilation. Additionally, there is rarely a great place to hang a towel to dry in your crowded dorm room or shared bathroom. Wet towels turn into stinky, musty towels in a hurry, and let's be honest, laundry doesn't happen often. Save the fluffy towels as a gift idea for college graduation!

The good news is that there are several affordable options for quick-dry towels, making them a much better choice for college life. I introduced the OEKO-TEX certification on page 63, and I encourage you to look for it on towels as well.

Where to Hang Towels to Dry in a Dorm Room

There are actually a few dorm rooms with towel bars on the walls, but they are few and far between.

Getting towels to dry in a dorm room is a challenge, as the best way is to spread them out with as little bunching as possible.

I do love quick-dry towels with a hanging loop, and if you don't have those, you can sew on a loop or run a hair band through the towel's tag to create a loop. This prevents any part of the towel from bunching over a hook. If you can pull the ends of the towel away from where the loop is mounted, that would be even better.

For a hook, check your dorm rules first and then select from over-the-door hooks, S-hooks, or heavy-duty adhesive hooks.

How Many Sets of Towels Does a College Student Need?

Keep in mind that space is limited, so consider how frequently your student will do laundry when determining how many towels to buy. If your student is accustomed to having a fresh towel every day, that may be a very tough standard to uphold in dorm life, given the space available or the frequency of doing laundry.

"How many sets of towels to bring?" is a frequently asked question in our dorm recommendations Facebook community, and the most common answer is two sets. However, each student should match their needs to the available space and expected laundry frequency.

BATHROOM ETIQUETTE—NO MATTER THE BATHROOM TYPE

Sharing bathrooms with a bunch of strangers, or even just with your best friend from high school, can lead to frustration and complaints.

Do your best to:

- Keep countertops clean
- Limit shower and mirror time
- Clean your hair out of drains and sinks
- Respect early and late hours
- Minimize the use of fragrance-producing products
- Hang your towels out of the way
- Replace empty toilet paper rolls

- Dispose of hygiene products and razors properly
- Establish a clear cleaning schedule and responsibilities from the start

Key Actions to Take

- ☐ **Research and confirm your dorm's bathroom type.**
- ☐ **Choose quick-dry towels.**
- ☐ **Plan for a drying area for wet caddies, shoes, and umbrellas.**
- ☐ **Expect (and plan for) a few quirks—every dorm has them.**
- ☐ **Ensure that all students have bathroom cleaning skills before leaving for college!**

16

Dorm Laundry & Cleaning

What You'll Take Away

- → How to navigate campus laundry rooms, apps, rules, and etiquette
- → Which laundry hamper is appropriate based on the location of the laundry room
- → How to get the drying cycle right the first time, and where to hang-dry clothing
- → A plan for a simple cleaning schedule based on a ten-minute weekly routine
- → The cleaning supplies you'll need and those to leave at home

Let's be honest: Very few people love doing laundry, and even fewer enjoy hauling a heavy laundry basket several floors (or buildings) away to do it. The reality is that laundry is part of adulting, and the easier it is to do, the more likely it is to actually happen.

What's something most young adults love even less than doing laundry? Cleaning!

This chapter will help make laundry and cleaning more manageable (and maybe even satisfying). You will feel a sense of accomplishment as you head back to the dorm room with fresh, clean sheets, towels, and clothes to start the school week off strong.

LAUNDRY 101 FOR DORM-BOUND COLLEGE STUDENTS

It may seem like there isn't much to learn about laundry, but stick with me here. Much of the college laundry preparation can be done at home in advance of heading off to college. In addition to doing your own laundry at home (practice!), work on labeling your important items, researching campus laundry rules, and consider your options for laundry hampers and baskets. Please note that there are often differences between the commercial machines at school and the ones you have at home—look into what current and former dorm residents have reported. In this chapter, you'll also find tips for sorting, loading, drying, and dewrinkling, as well as shared laundry room etiquette.

College Prerequisite: Laundry 101 at Home

If older high school students have not yet started doing their own laundry at home, now is the time to start. It is important to practice reading garment care tags, sorting clothes by color, separating towels and bulky items, and understanding the various machine cycles—not to mention how to handle a brand-new red shirt, and drying logistics such as when to hang-dry versus machine-dry. The more students familiarize themselves with the entire laundry routine, the more likely they are to do laundry regularly once they head off to college.

Label Your Belongings

It's always a good idea to subtly label your clothing.

You and your roommate might have the same black big-brand leggings or a trendy hoodie in the same size and color. Avoid any confusion by labeling your items with your initials using a permanent marker.

Research Your Campus Laundry Setup

Every school handles laundry differently. Some have machines on every floor, while others might require a short walk across campus. Most schools use an app or reloadable ID card for payment—rarely coins—and many specify which detergents are allowed (some ban detergent sheets, pods, or dryer sheets). If you have trouble finding the details, check your housing website or ask your RA.

Pro Tip: Liquid detergent bottles are heavy and cumbersome, so I recommend purchasing a smaller bottle to take to the laundry room and refilling it as necessary from a bigger bottle kept in the room.

Laundry Hampers (for Dirty Clothes)

Determine the location of your laundry facilities before selecting a style of laundry hamper/laundry basket for your dorm room. The location really will make a difference.

Laundry Room Location and Hamper Style

- Wheeled Hampers: Good for laundry facilities at a distance, and if there are no stairs involved to get there.
- Wheeled Tote Bags: Another option for laundry facilities at a distance, and easier to lift and carry if a couple of steps are involved.
- Laundry Backpack: Ideal for navigating stairs or long walks across campus. Models with a frame that can stand on their own are helpful.
- Pop-Up Hamper: Their light weight and short straps make these more appropriate for nearby machines on the hall.

Laundry Hamper Size

Plan for a laundry hamper to hold at least two weeks' worth of laundry, keeping in mind a dorm-friendly hamper size, and consider where the laundry hamper will sit to help with selection. Look for laundry hampers that are at least 70 liters/18 gallons.

Special Considerations

For athletes, animal science majors, and culinary students, consider a hamper with a lid to minimize smells in the dorm room. Odor-absorbing hanging bags in the closet may also be helpful.

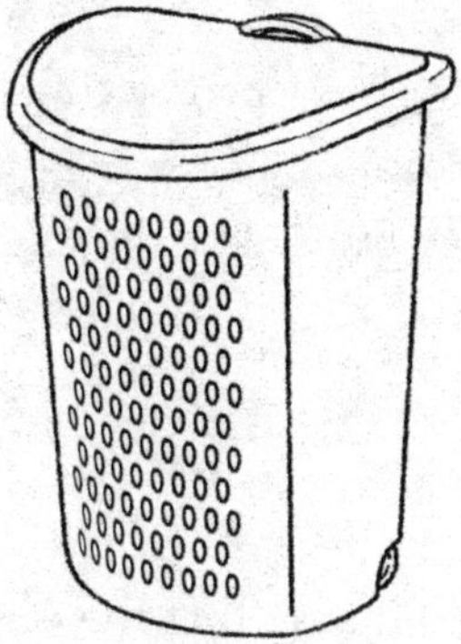

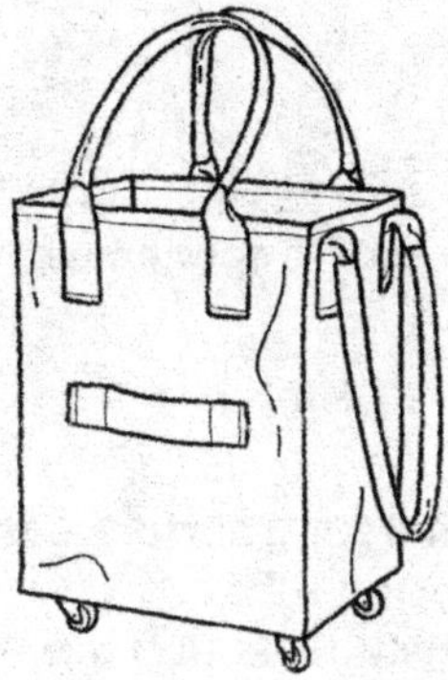

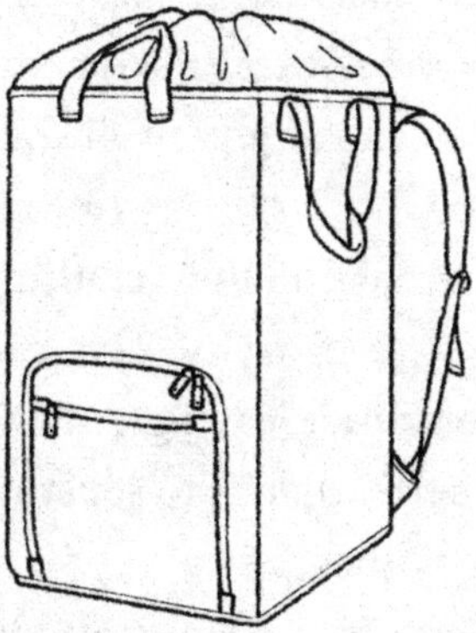

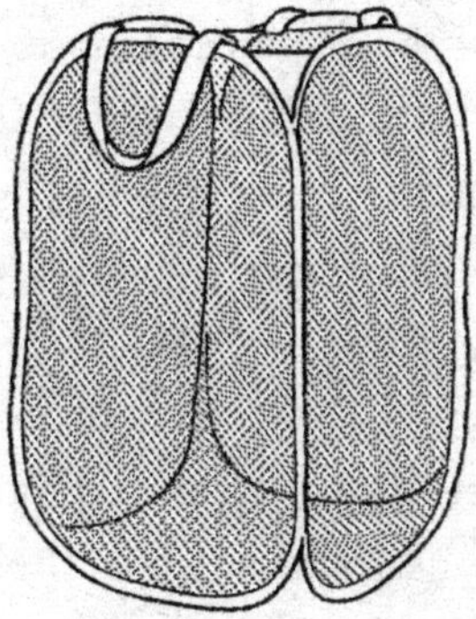

Laundry Baskets (for Clean Clothes)

I prefer not to put clean clothes back in a dirty laundry hamper, but having a separate laundry hamper and laundry basket in a dorm situation may be a lot to ask. If you decide to bring clean clothes back to the room in a separate container, consider using a standard plastic laundry basket if you have the storage space. Alternatively, you could use a collapsible laundry basket, an open tote, or even a moving bag for easy carrying.

Given the limited space for a laundry basket, it is essential to establish the habit of folding and hanging clothes immediately upon returning to the room. It takes only a couple of minutes!

Pro Tip: Pair doing laundry with listening to a podcast or studying to create a routine. A weekly notes review and organization session while doing laundry is a great plan.

Detergent, Sorting, Loading, and Cycles

As students prepare to do laundry, they should note that the campus laundry room has commercial washing machines. The water probably doesn't get extremely hot, the machines won't have many cycles, and it's hard to see inside to ensure that you've gotten all your items out.

To speed up laundry, students may try to make all their clothing fit into one washing machine, filling it to over capacity. This can cause the detergent not to fully dissolve or rinse, leaving residue inside the drum, on the clothes, or both. A better plan is to separate bulk items, such as sheets and towels, from clothes.

The following are tips for successful laundry sessions at college:

- Check the machine *before* loading to ensure that there is no residue or a bright red sock left behind from the last cycle.
- Clearly understand what detergents are permitted.
- Keep a stain-removing pen handy with your laundry supplies.
- Use mesh laundry/lingerie bags to protect your favorite T-shirts, leggings, and other delicate items. Also use them to keep socks in check.
- Ditch the fabric softener. It can also leave a layer of residue on your clothes and reduce the absorption of your towels.

Machine Drying and Air-Drying

While throwing the entire load of laundry in the dryer may be the easiest option, it is likely not ideal for all your items. As with the commercial washing machines, the commercial dryers probably won't have many cycles, especially a delicate cycle.

The following are tips for drying clothes while living in a dorm room:

- Shake items before putting them in the dryer to release bunched and tangled items, reduce wrinkles, and potentially shorten drying times.
- Pull out quick-dry items early to prevent overdrying and allow bulkier items to dry more quickly.
- Consider a drying rack for your room that best suits your layout. Options include a folding floor rack, a tall hanging rack, and an over-the-door hanging rack.
- If dryer sheets are not permitted or desired, consider using wool dryer balls to help reduce static, speed the dry cycle, and maintain softness.

Dewrinkling Clothes

Students are often surprised by how often they must wear business or formal attire in college. You'll need a way to keep your clothes looking professional; you might suddenly use them for club meetings, mock interviews, internships, job fairs, and social formals.

Irons are often on the "do not bring" list, but garment steamers may be permitted. These are easier to use and do not require space for an ironing board.

Many students bring wrinkle-release spray and try as hard as possible to use this over any sort of heat-involved dewrinklers!

Laundry Room Etiquette

There are many complaints about shared laundry facilities every year. You can't change the washers and dryers, but you can contribute to a happier and more efficient laundry space. Here are some helpful tips:

- Set timers or notifications to remind you to promptly unload machines if you leave the laundry room while your items are in the washer or dryer.
- Double-check your machines to ensure that no one's garments were left behind and that you're not leaving any items behind. Socks are hard to see in top loaders.
- If your laundry room lacks a designated lost and found area, consider setting one up!

KEEPING THE DORM ROOM CLEAN AND NEAT

Now that we've established a plan for successful laundry runs and clean clothes, let's shift to keeping the dorm room clean.

A cramped dorm room is so much better when it is neat and clean! Desk clutter can reduce interest in using the desk for studying. Food and refrigerator clutter can lead to spending more money on less healthy food. Sheets that really need to be changed don't make for a good night's sleep. It doesn't take much effort to maintain a space that allows students to focus on studying and productivity.

There are also health and safety reasons to keep the room neat. Unwashed dishes, damp towels, and sweaty clothes piled up on the floor can lead to mildew or even mold. Dust can trigger allergies and asthma. Having a place for everything—even if bins and drawers need to be labeled—is a must.

And don't forget pest prevention. Pests are notorious in dorms—there are so many delicious crumbs, open sugary drink bottles, overflowing trash cans, and appealing sticky spills. Don't give insects or rodents a reason to visit your room!

Pro Tip: As with laundry, be sure cleaning skills are well-established at home before leaving for college.

Establish a Decluttering and Cleaning Routine

A specific plan should be developed between the roommates, but this is a good guide to get you started.

Daily:

- **Mini Kitchen:** Clean up crumbs and sticky spots, and check the floor below as well.
- **Microwave:** Wipe the interior after use and clean the splatter cover regularly.
- **Food:** Store nonrefrigerated food in an airtight container.
- **Clothes:** Put all clean clothes away and place dirty clothes in the laundry hamper.
- **Shoes:** Straighten your shoes and find a home for lesser-worn pairs.
- **Wet Items:** Spread out your bath towel to dry; give your damp umbrella and shoes a spot to dry off.

Weekly—the Ten-Minute Reset

- **Desk Clutter:** Remove accumulated items from the desk; it often becomes the catch-all spot.
- **New Items:** Establish a home for new items brought into the room, and store lesser-used items in secondary storage areas.
- **Surfaces:** Do a quick wipe of the tops of the desk, dresser, and nightstand, and of the fridge and microwave handles.
- **Fresh Air:** If possible, open the window to air out the room.
- **Floors:** Vacuum the entire room. If needed, sprinkle a little baking soda over the rug or carpet, let it sit for at least 15 minutes to freshen it up, and then vacuum.
- **Fridge:** Remove any expired food or drinks.
- **Trash:** Take trash and recycling to designated areas.

Monthly

- **Bath/Shower:** Remove items from the shower caddy, give it a quick wipe-down, and allow it to dry fully.
- **Floors:** Mop any exposed hard surfaces after vacuuming.
- **Clothes:** Cycle any clothes to off-season storage as appropriate.
- **Fridge:** Wipe down shelves and drawers.
- **Surfaces:** Wipe down any permanent surfaces, such as window ledges and built-in shelving.
- **Appliances:** Clean interiors; check filters and other removable or replaceable parts.
- **Air Purifier:** Check the filter; it will likely need to be replaced at least once during the school year.
- **Water Filter Pitchers:** Check the filter if it doesn't have an automatic indicator.

- **Fans:** If the blades and insides are covered in dust, take them outside and use a can of compressed air to blow it off.

Extras for Private Bathrooms and Kitchens

- **Bathrooms:** Create a schedule for the roommates to share bathroom cleaning, including the sink, faucet, handles, counter, mirror, toilet, shower, and floor.
- **Shower:** Check the shower curtain liner for mold or mildew; these liners are inexpensive to replace.
- **Kitchen:** Wipe down counters, the stovetop, tables, and the inside of the microwave.
- **Living Room:** Declutter and wipe off tables.
- **Fridge:** Remove any expired food or drinks.
- **Floors:** Mop bathroom and kitchen floors, and other hard-surface flooring.

Cleaning Supplies for a Dorm Room

As with other items you're bringing to the room, please check with your roommates about scented items, including cleaning supplies. Scents can trigger migraines and allergies, and cleaning can be done just as well without them.

Unless you have a cabinet in the room, use a plastic caddy, a plastic bin, a shelf on a utility cart, or an over-the-door hanger to store the cleaning supplies.

You Will Need:

- Multi-surface cleaner or wipes
- Paper towels
- A small stick vacuum and/or a mini broom/dustpan, depending on the floor surfaces. Check with your dorm to see if

vacuum cleaners are available for checkout, but don't expect them to be very effective.

- A sponge, dish soap, and a kitchen drying towel. Kitchen towels will also need to be cleaned regularly in the washing machine.
- Water bottle brush, and skinny drinking straw brush. Consider using denture cleaning tabs to make cleaning your water bottle easier.
- Garbage bags for the main trash can and any smaller trash cans
- For private baths: shower and sink cleaner, glass cleaner, mop with wet pads or cleaner, toilet brush or toilet wand cleaning system

What Not to Bring

- Harsh or heavily scented cleaners or bleach
- Aerosol sprays; these are often prohibited in dorms
- Plug-in or other scent diffusers
- Oversized upright vacuums or big mops with buckets that require larger storage areas

Key Actions to Take

- [ ] **Research your dorm's laundry locations and rules.**
- [ ] **Practice doing laundry and properly cleaning before leaving for college, so you are an expert upon arrival.**
- [ ] **Pick a hamper based on your laundry route (stairs/elevator/distance) and decide whether a separate clean-clothes carrier is desired.**

- [ ] Plan for small laundry solutions: a smaller bottle for liquid detergent or sheets, and a stain-removing pen. Many laundry hampers have pouches for these items.
- [ ] Set a designated laundry time and plan to use that time to review notes and study.
- [ ] Plan for a ten-minute weekly room reset; consistency is more important than perfection.
- [ ] Follow the checklists for the daily, weekly, and monthly cleaning suggestions.
- [ ] Choose simple, nontoxic cleaning products that are easy to store in a caddy. Start getting used to using them before leaving for college.

17

Air Quality, Comfort & Temperatures

What You'll Take Away

- → Why sniffles and lingering colds spike in fall semester dorms—and when to look beyond germs to air quality
- → How to spot potential mold issues (even when they aren't visible) and what to do about them
- → How to choose, place, and maintain an air purifier sized for a typical dorm room
- → When to add dehumidifiers or moisture absorbers, and when a humidifier actually helps
- → How to make temperatures more comfortable even when there is no (working) thermostat in the room

College freshmen face many challenges as they begin their college career: a new home, a new roommate, new food, new freedoms, an academic wake-up call (for most), and the big task of finding their people. It's a lot. One thing families may not consider is the unwelcome challenge of battling sniffles and recurring illnesses shortly after school starts. Remember kindergarten? It's like that again.

When it comes to college, though, it isn't only the germs congregating in small dorm rooms, university buses, and crowded dining halls that lead to illnesses. Students often aren't sleeping enough, aren't eating well, and probably aren't taking those multivitamins tucked into their first aid kit. And are they hydrating?

Colds and congestion are very common in the fall. Hopefully, it doesn't get to a point where the student misses classes—college is already more challenging than high school, and even more so with missed days.

If those sniffles and coughs persist, however, you might consider air quality and potential mold exposure as possible culprits, too.

HOW FREQUENTLY IS MOLD AN ISSUE IN DORM ROOMS?

Mold is a fungus that thrives in environments that are damp and warm, and dorms are notoriously both. The primary zones of concern include the areas near the window HVAC units, near small attached bathrooms, and inside the ceiling vents. Mold can also grow in bathroom exhaust fans, in shower stalls and on shower curtains, under sinks, and in corners where damp towels pile up. Carpets or rugs that are not dried quickly after spills, and humid closets, can also be targets.

The problem with mold in college dorms is that you may feel the effects before you actually see it, especially if it's inside vents, behind drywall, or in a tall, unlit closet. Old buildings, poor air circulation, condensation inside air vents, regional humidity, and several steamy showers a day in tiny bathrooms all add up. It isn't only a problem in older buildings, either—newer construction can have issues if ventilation or moisture management is poor.

SIGNS THAT THERE COULD BE MOLD IN THE DORM ROOM

You may not be able to see mold if it's inside vents or behind walls. Therefore, be aware of the following signs that may indicate mold growth. For any physical symptoms, consult a medical professional.

- Persistent, musty odors with no clear source
- Unexplained damp surfaces or walls that feel soft when pressed
- Discoloration on walls or belongings: black, brown, green, powdery white, blue, or slimy textures are common indicators of mold
- Dark water stains on ceilings, walls, or floors
- Headaches or migraines that feel different than usual*
- Difficulty breathing, coughing, shortness of breath, or wheezing*
- Rash, hives, itching, runny nose, or sneezing*

* SOURCE: CDC, July 2023, www.cdc.gov/niosh/mold/health-problems/?CDC_AAref_Val=https://www.cdc.gov/niosh/topics/indoorenv/moldsymptoms.html.

WHAT STUDENTS SHOULD DO IF THEY SUSPECT MOLD

If a student isn't feeling well and has symptoms of mold exposure, they should seek medical care. Testing can rule out common viruses; if symptoms persist, take additional steps.

Students should report concerns to the university immediately. Begin by contacting the RA or the housing department. Students should document each mold-related conversation and keep copies of incident reports filed online. This is a good learning opportunity; students should advocate for themselves, handle reporting, and follow up.

If the response is insufficient, the student should escalate the issue within the university or consider contacting the local health department for assistance.

HOW TO FIGHT GERMS AND POSSIBLE MOLD-RELATED ILLNESS

The good news? You can reduce risks from mold, germs, and odors with simple appliances and habits.

An air purifier pulls in room air and runs it through a filter to capture particles such as bacteria, dust, smoke, mold spores, and pollen, then circulates cleaner air back into the room. The filters in air purifiers need regular checks and occasional replacement. Expect to replace a dorm air purifier filter at least once, and possibly multiple times, during the school year, depending on air quality.

We've heard many accounts from families whose students stayed sick through the entire fall semester. After doctor visits, rounds of antibiotics, and lots of head-scratching, someone suggests trying an air purifier—and often there's a noticeable improvement. A quick search for "mold in dorms" turns up plenty of photos and reports.

A dehumidifier adds another layer of protection in humid climates or in rooms that feel continually damp. It removes moisture from the air and helps keep surfaces dry. An unexpected bonus? Snacks and cereal stay crunchy when the room's moisture is reduced.

WHAT TO LOOK FOR IN AIR PURIFIERS FOR DORM ROOMS

- **Room Size Coverage:** Most dorm rooms are 150 to 225 square feet (with exceptions). Choose a purifier that can recirculate every twelve to fifteen minutes, based on your room's square footage. Many listings advertise square footage per hour, so you'll need to dig into the details of the single-cycle rate to ensure that comparisons are apples to apples.
- **Filtration:** Look for True HEPA or HEPA systems.
- **Particle Size:** Mold spores and some bacteria can be one to three microns; ensure that the filter captures particles in that range.
- **Avoid Ozone-Producing Modes:** Skip UV/ionizer models that generate ozone.
- **Noise Level:** No model is silent; a little white noise can be helpful. Discuss settings with your roommate.
- **Filter Costs and Availability:** Dorm conditions can shorten filter life. Check availability and set a reminder to inspect the filter around Thanksgiving (earlier on dusty or pollen-heavy campuses).
- **Smart/App Features:** Campus Wi-Fi often blocks smart devices. Don't choose a model only for its smart features unless you plan to reuse it off campus later.
- **Built-In Night-Lights:** Handy when roommates keep different

hours—make sure the light can be turned off for true darkness.

Pro Tip: Visit TheDormGuide.com for our up-to-date air purifier comparisons and recommendations for dorm rooms and apartments.

WHERE TO PUT AN AIR PURIFIER IN A DORM ROOM

In a crowded dorm room, it is challenging to position an air purifier exactly where you need it, but the best spot is as close as possible to the most likely source of contaminants. Often, that's up high near a supply vent, which means placing the purifier on a desk hutch, an over-fridge shelf, or the top of a wardrobe unit. In general, keep it as central in the room as possible, rather than in a corner, and give it a few inches of clearance around the intake and exhaust.

REDUCING DAMPNESS IN DORM ROOMS

As discussed in several chapters of this book, dampness and humidity are common complaints in dorm rooms across the country, even in drier climates. While this dampness may just cause soggy snacks and towels that take forever to dry, it can also lead to an environment ripe for mold and mildew.

A dehumidifier lowers humidity by collecting moisture from the air. In-home dehumidifiers are usually connected to a drain and can run with minimal intervention. However, this is not possible in a dorm room, so if you decide to add one to your dorm room, you'll need a portable dehumidifier with a water collection chamber.

Portable dehumidifier models have chambers as small as 16 ounces, but speaking from experience, try to find one with a larger chamber. My son's dehumidifier has an 85-ounce water chamber, and he needs to empty it into a sink about every other day. Most of these models will automatically shut off when the chamber is full, so the larger the chamber, the longer it will run between emptying. For the best results, consider incorporating emptying the water chamber into the daily routine, such as when the student gets ready for bed and heads to the sink.

Where powered units aren't practical or allowed, moisture absorbers (bucket or hanging styles) can help in closets, under sinks, or in other problem zones. Once these absorbers are full of water, they will need to be replaced.

WHEN DORM ROOMS ARE TOO DRY

Dorm rooms that are too dry are less common, but they can occur in any climate. The dryness is more frequently associated with the constant running of the heat or air-conditioning than with a dry climate.

When dryness causes health concerns such as dry skin, chapped lips, and nosebleeds, humidifiers add moisture to the air in these very dry rooms. They're also helpful to soothe colds and congestion. Choose a model that can be filled from a water bottle, as you may not be able to fill it under a faucet. Additionally, look for parts that are easy to remove and clean, and avoid adding essential oils unless your roommate agrees (many students are sensitive to fragrances).

IS THERE ONE APPLIANCE THAT HANDLES ALL THE AIR ISSUES?

This is a common question in our community. Given that dorm rooms are small and already crowded, it is a good question whether combining these functions into one appliance is feasible.

Unfortunately, while there are a couple of products on the market that claim to be two-in-one air purifiers and dehumidifiers, these products struggle to perform two different functions and have low ratings because they don't handle either function well.

DORM ROOM TEMPERATURES

We've covered air quality and humidity, but what about controlling the temperature in a dorm room?

This varies from school to school and even by room within the same hall. Some schools have thermostats in the rooms—you may spot one in photos—but they may have been disconnected long ago. In some cases, they are operational and allow you to control the temperature, but most students find that adjusting the temperature setting doesn't make much of a difference.

If the Room Is Too Warm

This is the most frequent complaint, and it is definitely widespread. The answer is almost always fans.

If the room's window opens, consider placing a box fan in the open window to pull warm air out of the room.

Most students bring a desk fan to their dorm. While it is called a desk fan due to its size, it is often placed close to the bed, blowing on the student to cool them while they sleep. The most popular model for dorms is a compact fan with 360-degree oscillation, designed to maximize air movement. Tower fans can also be used to maintain airflow throughout the room.

Consider fan noise when selecting fans for college. Some students appreciate a noisy fan to help drown out hallway noise, outdoor noise, and even the snoring of their roommates. Some students want the room to be quiet. This is a good conversation to have with roommates before moving in.

Beyond using fans, consider closing blinds or using curtains to block the sun's rays when they shine through the window during the day. Also consider using 100 percent cotton breathable bedding layers, as cotton is much cooler than microfiber (a polyester that is frequently marketed to students because it is soft).

If the Room Is Too Cold

Almost all campuses prohibit the use of space heaters in campus housing. If the room is too cold and the temperature cannot be adjusted, ask the RA for suggestions or to escalate the issue to the housing department. Extra bedding layers, fuzzy socks, slippers, wearable blankets, and warm beverages can help, too!

AIR QUALITY BEYOND THE DORM YEARS

Air-quality issues aren't limited to dorm rooms. After dorm life, most students move to older, budget-friendly apartments or houses. Poor air quality, germs, and roommate cooking adventures are all good reasons to continue using an air purifier in your bedroom.

In humid regions, a dehumidifier can also make rooms feel more comfortable without needing to lower the AC temperature. In dry climates or areas where the heat is constantly running, a humidifier can be beneficial.

Fans will always be a good idea. You may not agree with your roommates' temperature choices, or you may need to block traffic noise or noise within your own apartment.

PRACTICE BEFORE MOVE-IN DAY

I recommend unboxing these appliances before move-in, reading the setup instructions, and putting the appliances to use. The more familiar students are with the use and maintenance of these appliances, the more likely they are to use them correctly. It is also a good time to verify that the items are working correctly while you are still in the return window. Be sure to hold on to the boxes and protective packaging for move-in day.

- **Air Purifier:** Make sure the filter isn't wrapped in plastic inside the machine. The student should read the instructions for removing and reinstalling the filter. Turn it on and let it run on different settings.
- **Dehumidifier:** Read the setup instructions, then plug it in and let it work. Practice pulling out the water chamber, emptying it, and then replacing it.
- **Humidifier:** Add water to the tank, plug it in, and let it run.

If any of these appliances are smart, connect to the app to learn their functionality. Note that Wi-Fi-only appliances may not be able to connect to your campus network, so it is a good idea to also learn how to use the appliances in manual mode.

Key Actions to Take

- [ ] Start researching air quality issues on campus or particular dorms that you're likely to live in—look for parent Facebook groups, Instagram housing accounts, Reddit, and general internet searches.
- [ ] Discuss temperature preferences, fans, and white noise with roommates.
- [ ] Divide the list of necessary appliances among roommates if you decide to bring multiple.

18

Dorm Room Decor

What You'll Take Away

- How to create a comfortable, personal dorm space without overspending or overbuying
- Which decor items are worth it (and which ones almost always disappoint)
- How to choose affordable, nontoxic materials for rugs, bedding, and wall decor
- Why it matters to coordinate early with your roommate
- How to plan decor that packs, travels, and resells well
- Why perfection on social media should *never* be the goal

SETTING THE STAGE: COMFORT OVER COMPETITION

Dorm decor is about comfort, personality, and function. While, yes, some students (and, let's be real, their parents) might go above and beyond, it is not about competition or social media validation. You don't need to hire a designer, and you definitely don't need a five-figure budget. In fact, the best dorm rooms often come together through a mix of thoughtful planning, casual coordination (as opposed to forced matching), personal touches, and affordable choices.

Honestly, the word *decor* is often overused when it comes to dorm rooms. What does decor include? Bedding? Rugs? Curtains? Wall art? Lamps? String lights? We can have all those things without needing a design board, let alone a designer.

Let the students create a space that feels like them, without concern for trends or cameras, and see what they come up with on their own. This is a great step toward adulting and making decisions that can actually begin the transition to college life.

Social Media Versus Real Life

Those perfectly styled dorm photos you see online? They're photographed right after move-in, before the late nights, the takeout containers, the laundry piles, the shoe sprawl, and the early burnout of making the beds every day. The goal isn't the first-day photo. The goal is to create a space that students feel confident maintaining and where they feel comfortable studying, relaxing, and getting some sleep.

THREE STEPS BEFORE YOU START SHOPPING

A blank-canvas room can be a fun challenge, but it can also be overwhelming. Begin with these three steps to get started on the right track with your decor plan.

Step 1: Start with the Rules

Before you begin planning, choosing a color scheme, or commissioning art, please do your research and check your housing rules (see page 9). Every school has unique rules, limitations, and restrictions, particularly regarding outside furniture, wall decor, and the use of rugs or curtains.

Some dorms prohibit the use of extension cords or plug-in string lights. Others don't allow curtains, nails, or even wall adhesives. You may not be able to bring a rug or hang curtains without proof of fire resistance, let alone hang wallpaper. Knowing the rules before you start planning saves time, money, and frustration on move-in day.

In addition to the long list of what is not allowed, most housing sites also provide room layouts with (hopefully!) measurements and furniture dimensions. Some schools offer 3D virtual tours of rooms, complete with online measuring tools, to assist with space planning.

Pro Tip: Most schools do not allow box trucks or U-Haul trailers on move-in day, so try to keep the amount, sizes, and weight of what's coming in reasonable. It will be hot, crowded, and messy on move-in day—I can promise you that.

Think through logistics. You have to get everything to school, either in a car, in a couple of cars, or maybe even on an airplane. And everything you bring in has to come back out about nine months later, when the student will take the lead on most of the packing as the school year winds down. Determining what will work again next year and reselling or donating items that won't takes a backseat to studying for finals, going to end-of-year parties, and finding a summer job. The result is often a panicked trip to the dumpster with perfectly useful items because the RA needs to sign off on an empty room.

Step 2: Coordinate with Roommates

Most students have at least one roommate, which often requires coordinating a layout and style plan with them. This should be done as early as possible; a decision not to coordinate at all is also absolutely acceptable. Roommates who choose to coordinate may do so casually around a theme or color palette, or go all in with matching bedding, headboards, neon signs, and desk setups.

Whether going their own way, coordinating, or matching, roommates should discuss shared items in the room—the things that you need only one of or that you are allowed to have only one of in the room per school restrictions (see page 76).

Step 3: Determine Your Design Inspiration

If you need a jumping-off point for the design of your dorm room, start with the one thing you know you want. Whether it's a theme, color palette, comforter, rug, or fun piece of wall art you already own, having that inspiration is helpful.

If that one thing you want is neutrals, then that's all you need to get started! Or maybe it is a jewel-tone-inspired scheme, a beach cottage vibe, or a retro look. You don't have to stick to the theme loyally; it just helps to have a direction.

If you are coordinating with your roommate, get agreement on that inspiration, and start making decisions.

BEDDING: THE BIGGEST STATEMENT ON YOUR SIDE OF THE ROOM

If your side of the dorm has a focal point, it's the bed. It's the most visible feature and takes up the most considerable portion of your side of the room. Whether you're going with a theme or a color scheme, try to settle on the bedding early. You might think it will be easy to find a purple floral comforter and build around that, only to find that you can't find purple floral anywhere. Planning early is best, and pay attention to return windows in case you see something you like better later on.

Focus on bedding that is washable, breathable, and durable. Dorm life and commercial laundry machines can be tough on bedding. If you're considering an expensive name-brand comforter or even a custom-made duvet, I recommend finding an affordable alternative that closely resembles your desired look.

Pro Tip: When it comes to pillows, less is more. A couple of bed pillows and one throw pillow at most. I regularly hear complaints about too many throw pillows, because there is nowhere to put them when it's time to go to sleep.

For all bedding, look for:

- Cotton over synthetics; cotton is cooler and more durable.
- OEKO-TEX certified materials, to ensure that there are no harmful chemicals in the bedding.
- Mix-and-match layers; layer blankets, throws, or pillows for pops of color or pattern.

RUGS: ADD FUNCTIONAL, AFFORDABLE WARMTH TO THE ROOM

As parents, most of us did not bring rugs to our dorm rooms. I sure didn't. But today students prefer dorm room floors to be covered.

There may be linoleum or carpet already in the room, and the rug you bring will live a rough year. Rugs add warmth and style instantly, but they'll be subjected to a year of icky shoes, crumbs, hair, dirt, and mystery spills in the dorm room.

There are so many great low-pile, even machine-washable rugs these days made with nontoxic materials; you're sure to find an excellent option for your room at an affordable price. Avoid fluffy or shag rugs altogether, though—they trap all the dirt, grime, crumbs, hair, and worse, and they're really hard to vacuum.

What is the best size rug for a dorm room?

This really depends on the room size and layout. For a standard double room, a 5-by-7- or 6-by-9-foot rug should cover the visible area between parallel beds. If the beds are fully lofted, you'll want a larger size to fill most of the space under the beds as well.

CURTAINS FOR DORM ROOMS

If permitted, curtains can make a dorm feel instantly more "finished." They add the illusion of height, as well as texture and coziness. However, be sure they're allowed—and installed in accordance with the rules.

The dorm room likely comes with metal blinds, which are helpful for privacy but not great at blocking light. If the blinds alone are sufficient for you, then skip right past this section.

You will not be permitted to drill or screw hardware into the dorm walls to hang a curtain rod. If the window is in a recessed opening (a square or rectangular cutout in the wall), a tension rod is a good solution.

> **Pro Tip:** Place a few pieces of painter's tape on the wall before putting up the tension rod. This can save you from accidentally peeling off years of paint layers when you remove the tension rod at the end of the school year.

If the window has a frame but not enough room for a tension rod, consider a curtain rod with tension mounts on the inside of the frame, positioned in front of the window.

If there isn't an opening for a tension rod, adhesive curtain hooks may be permitted. If using these, follow the directions carefully, including cleaning the walls before installation and allowing sufficient adhesion time between steps.

Choose light-filtering or blackout curtains based on your student's sleep and decor preferences. It is best to choose shorter curtains to hang just above an air vent or furniture below. Heavy curtains will put a strain on adhesive hooks.

WALL DECOR: WALL ART, MIRRORS, AND LIGHTS

Dorm walls are notoriously challenging to decorate. Most dorms prohibit nails or heavy-duty anchors, but a few with Sheetrock surfaces may allow small tacks. Dorms with plaster or cinder block walls will likely only have the option of adhesive hangers or painter's tape.

Note that some schools have restrictions on hanging items at a minimum distance from the ceiling or covering a maximum percentage of the wall space. Please consult the dorm rules before making a plan. Some dorms also offer corkboard strips or large rectangles for hanging your wall decor. In this case, bring plenty of tacks to hang your items.

For any of these situations, though, lightweight is the only way to go for wall decor.

- Prints or posters, if framed, should be framed in lightweight poster frames with plexiglass or acrylic fronts. These appear to be glass but are actually lightweight and shouldn't shatter if the print slides off the wall.
- Corkboards or pegboards should be lightweight and handled with care when adding or removing items.
- Flags and tapestries should be lightweight—consider adding loops or hooks to the back if they are not built into the fabric.
- Bulky canvas art or mirrors that require hanging should not be used in a dorm room.

Pro Tip: Choose lightweight, shatter-resistant wall decor for a dorm room.

If you are considering a full-length mirror, check with the school, as some have pre-installed mirrors on the backs of dorm or closet doors, or on a wall in the room. If this is not the case, consider bringing an inexpensive, lightweight over-the-door mirror.

Light strips, string lights, and neon lights are popular dorm decor items, but many dorms have specific restrictions or outright bans on them. If they are allowed, make sure you understand the guidelines for hanging them on the walls.

DESK DECOR

The desk is another thing you will notice in those heavily decorated dorm rooms—or actually, you might not, because the students do such a good job of hiding it with decor.

You can add simple decor to the desk with a desk mat, a faux succulent, a desk lamp, or bins and baskets in the desk hutch above, if you have one.

Others take it a step further by covering the desktop with cut-to-size fabric, wallpaper, or wrapping paper, then placing a fitted piece of acrylic on top. This hides the well-used desktop from view and also provides a protective surface.

To fully cover the desk, students drape fabric over it and then place a piece of acrylic on the desktop to keep the fabric in place. In these situations, they often change out the desk chair as well to match the decor. This is a more expensive undertaking, but if it is a priority, it can be done reasonably.

While covering or decorating the desk is not necessary, the acrylic topper is a nice option to make the desktop easier to clean.

As mentioned earlier, the dorm room desk chair is sometimes stowed away for the school year (somewhere in the dorm room, as it typically cannot be removed from the room) and replaced with a more comfortable desk chair. In other cases, the dorm room chair can be dressed up with a chair cover, a fuzzy blanket, or even a small fuzzy throw rug draped over the back and seat of the chair.

DORM ROOM LIGHTING

As discussed in chapter 13, task and ambient lighting make a huge difference in a dorm room. Being able to skip that harsh overhead light and use a task light, a floor lamp, or even a night-light can mean the difference between a good night's sleep and being kept awake—or even awakened—by harsh fluorescent lights.

Add affordable lighting in the room through:

- A desk lamp for focused light
- A clip-on or bedside lamp for reading
- Plug-in string lights (if allowed) for warmth
- Battery-powered LED puck lights under a desk hutch or a fully lofted bed

DECOR THAT DOES DOUBLE DUTY

Small spaces require smart planning for pieces that marry form and function and can even serve multiple roles. These items may include:

- Fun fabric ottomans that serve as a convenient step up to the bed and provide extra seating

- Colorful rolling carts for storing snacks, supplies, and more
- Baskets that look decorative but hide clutter or snacks
- Under-bed bins in coordinated colors to visually "extend" decor
- Closet curtains that coordinate with the room's decor while providing a cover for an open closet

THE COST OF OVERDOING IT

Let's pause for a quick reality check before making any decisions.

Most students move into their dorms in August and move out in May. That is nine months. Subtract about a month for winter break, another week for spring break, and time off for Thanksgiving and other holidays, and students may actually reside in that room for a total of only seven and a half months.

Every August and September, social media is flooded with photos of dorm rooms that resemble boutique hotel suites, complete with custom headboards, monogrammed bedding, matching drapery, and coordinated peel-and-stick wallpaper—and costing thousands of dollars in designer fees and fabrics.

There's no judgment here if that's someone's choice, but please know that these rooms you see on social media are the exception. They just get a lot of feedback, so you'll see them in your feed. None of it is necessary, and without proper planning, much of it becomes unusable or unwanted after those nine months.

For students who will live in dorms throughout college and can put those items to good use year after year, that's great; however, after one year on campus, many students move to apartments, houses, or upperclassmen on-campus housing with completely different layouts. Also consider that styles evolve, and what looked perfect when you were eighteen might feel dated a year later.

Among peers, ultra-luxury dorm setups sometimes have an unintended negative effect. Instead of garnering admiration, they can feel unrelatable or intimidating. Students who can't afford to "compete" may simply move on socially.

Pro Tip: Be yourself! If the decor makes the student feel relaxed, inspired, and at home, it's perfect. If it's only meant to impress on social media, consider shifting to comfort and functionality.

PLANNING FOR THE END OF THE YEAR

Every May, dumpsters outside college dorms overflow with rugs, curtains, carts, drawers, clothes, and decor that were used for less than a year. Some even still have tags. It is so wasteful. And completely preventable.

Encourage your student to think about what happens next before they buy:

- Can this item be reused in an apartment?
- Will it fit in a car or storage unit at year-end?
- Is it washable?

When it is time for move-out planning (at least one month in advance), the student should ask themself:

- Which items will I not use again and would rather not transport home?
- Can these items be recycled, resold, or donated?

If the school doesn't have a donation process at the end of the school year, the student could look into starting one. What a great addition to their résumé that would be!

Many campuses now host "move-out markets" where students can donate or swap gently used items. Facebook Marketplace, Buy Nothing groups, and campus resale pages are also great places to resell or donate unwanted items.

Please consider waste, sustainability, and helping others as the school year draws to a close.

EMOTIONAL DESIGN (AND LETTING GO)

This might be the hardest part for parents—especially for moms who have poured love into creating beautiful spaces at home and derive some of their sense of identity from that. It's natural to want their student's dorm room to reflect the same care and attention to detail.

But your student's dorm doesn't need to look like *your* home or represent you. It needs to feel like *their* space. This is college, it is expensive, and there will be more years in other housing that needs to be furnished and decorated. Starting at a really high baseline sets a bar for the rest of the college years and into the on-your-own years that may be challenging to maintain.

If the student loves mismatched posters, LED lights, and a beanbag chair, that's okay. If they prefer minimal neutrals and one framed photo, that's okay, too. What matters most is that *they* feel comfortable in the room.

Parents sometimes decorate to manage their own emotions—to soften the sting of goodbye, to feel they're still part of the process, to show love through design. That's understandable. But the best gift you can give your student is creative independence. Be their sounding board, but let them take the lead.

Let them have ownership of their space, even if it's not your style. You can still help them shop wisely, avoid overspending, and choose nontoxic, durable materials. You can remind them that comfort and connection matter far more than aesthetics.

And when you step back after move-in and see that tiny room through teary eyes, remember that this is where the next chapter of their life begins. It isn't at all about how it looks, but about how it feels.

Key Actions to Take

- ☐ **Read dorm housing rules before buying decor.**
- ☐ **Coordinate early with your roommate on colors, shared items, and budgets.**
- ☐ **Focus on functional comfort: bedding, a rug, lighting, and small touches.**
- ☐ **Choose affordable, washable, and nontoxic materials.**
- ☐ **Skip designer decor—one year in a dorm doesn't justify the investment.**
- ☐ **Be mindful of social and environmental impact when decorating.**
- ☐ **Plan for move-out with reuse, resale, or donation in mind.**
- ☐ **Let the student lead—this is *their* first home away from home.**

19

Bringing a Car to College

What You'll Take Away

- → How to decide if your student really needs a car at school
- → What to know about parking permits, timelines, rules, and extra costs
- → Safety, maintenance, and responsibility tips for college drivers
- → What to keep in the car for emergencies and convenience
- → How to handle storage during breaks
- → How you can potentially save on insurance if you leave the car at home

SHOULD YOU BRING A CAR TO COLLEGE?

Some students genuinely need to bring a car to school, particularly those who commute to college, have an off-campus job, or live farther from campus. However, for those in big cities, a car is almost certainly unnecessary and would be a hassle and a significant expense to have on campus.

If you're somewhere in the middle and not sure whether to take a car, this chapter will help lay out considerations to help you make a more informed decision.

Questions to consider:

- Does the college allow students, particularly freshmen, to have cars on campus?
- What are the campus transportation options? Bus service, shuttles? Are these included in mandatory student fees?
- Can on-campus students get to shopping on foot or via public transportation?
- Are ridesharing services readily available in the area?
- How much does on-campus parking cost?
- What are the on-campus parking options? Dorm buildings typically don't have plentiful adjacent parking, so remote overflow lots may be the only option. These lots are potentially too far to walk to from campus, and a shuttle may be required.
- Does the student have an older sibling with a car on campus or know that their roommate will bring a car?

With the answers to these questions in mind, proceed through this chapter for more information about bringing a car to college.

CAMPUS PARKING 101

Every school is different, but these are common issues and considerations for many schools.

Parking Permit Timing and Process

Depending on the school, obtaining parking permits may be a complicated and time-sensitive process. Some schools have lotteries for on-site parking; others allow you to apply based on when you applied to the school or when you paid your enrollment deposit. Some have plenty of parking, and you can decide at the last minute. The key is to find out early so you can take these steps if needed.

If your student does bring a car, the first lesson is learning where it can—and can't—be parked. Most colleges require students to register their vehicle and display a parking pass. Permits can sell out early, so applying as soon as the portal opens is key.

If the student goes home for long breaks and won't take their car, check whether the school allows cars to remain on campus or if they must be stored elsewhere during breaks.

Know the Zones

If only I had a dollar for every time a friend complained to me about their student's college parking tickets. Schools take the rules seriously, and ticketing is a common occurrence. Be aware of overnight rules, which may differ from those for early-morning and daytime hours, as well as "move-your-car" mandates during major campus events, such as home football weekends.

Encourage your student to read the fine print about rules, time limits, and restricted zones. Some campuses ticket aggressively for parking in visitor or faculty lots, expired meters, or staying in a space overnight. A single semester of tickets can cost more than the permit itself.

And these zones aren't only important on campus! In fact, parking rules can be more confusing when parking off-campus. Towing can be common *and* almost immediate if you park illegally.

Pro Tip: Screenshot the campus parking map and save it as a favorite on your phone.

ARE THERE OFF-CAMPUS PARKING OPTIONS?

For students who can't or choose not to get a campus spot, off-campus parking might be an option. Nearby apartment complexes or churches may rent parking spaces to students, though safety and lighting should be considered before signing up.

Be sure to read all the fine print in parking contracts, including timeframe (full year or school year), ability to leave the car for breaks or long weekends, security measures in place, and access to video monitoring footage.

Pro Tip: Some insurance apps reward safe driving with lower premiums after a few months—worth activating before the semester starts.

CAR SAFETY AND SECURITY

College parking lots can be busy, poorly lit, and lack security, so it's worth reinforcing some simple car-safety and theft prevention habits.

- Lock the doors every time you get in or out of the car, even if you're just running back into the dorm for a minute.
- Remove all valuables from the car, including backpacks and bags. In high-crime areas, leave the glove box open to show that there are no valuables inside.
- Consider anti-theft add-ons, such as a steering wheel lock or a dash cam.
- Use Apple AirTags or Tile trackers to help locate a car in a large lot—or if it's ever moved without permission. These should be placed in a discreet location.
- Use apps to record your last parked location. Both Google Maps and Apple Maps offer parking locator options, as does Waze.
- Keep a set of spare keys in a secure location (not in the car or lying around in the dorm room). Refer to page 111 for recommendations for locking storage in a dorm room.

A special shout-out for dash cams: I am a huge fan of these, especially for younger and older drivers who are often wrongly assigned fault in an accident. While having a dash cam in a car will not lower insurance rates, being able to prove lack of fault or provide evidence to investigators as a witness to an incident is important.

Pro Tip: Have a family talk about who is responsible for gas, tickets, insurance, and repairs. Also discuss boundaries, including who can borrow the car, who can't, and how far the vehicle can be driven. Adulting has different meanings to different people, and waking up to find that your student is 300 miles away at a beach for the weekend may not be your definition of using the car responsibly.

PEER PRESSURE

When you are the student on the hall with a car, you may be repeatedly asked for rides, favors, or to drive everyone to the big festival in the next town over. This involves a lot of responsibility, wear and tear on the car, and the potential to be pressured into carrying more passengers than the seat belts allow or to rush to destinations. A lot is going on during freshman year of college, so consider this carefully before bringing a car and adding to commitments and social issues.

In addition to being a regular driver, loaning the car to friends may seem harmless, but it can get complicated. If someone else damages your car or is involved in an accident, your family's insurance usually pays—check your permissive use stipulations. Parking tickets and other violations also become a hassle. Ensure that students understand this and have a practiced way to decline when a friend asks to borrow their car.

CAR MAINTENANCE AWAY FROM HOME

Before the student leaves for college, schedule a comprehensive checkup that includes an oil change, new wiper blades, a tire inspection, a brake inspection, and fluid top-offs. A fresh start reduces the odds of mid-semester car repairs or maintenance.

Once on campus, the car may sit for days or weeks. Encourage short weekly drives to keep the battery healthy and prevent tires from developing flat spots.

Does the car, a membership, or your insurance plan include free towing or roadside assistance? Be sure everyone in the family knows how to use it when needed and whom to contact first if multiple options are available.

> **Pro Tip:** Set digital reminders for oil changes and inspections on a shared family calendar. Out of sight shouldn't mean out of mind.

END-OF-SEMESTER STORAGE AND BREAKS

When the semester wraps up, students often fly or carpool home for winter break, leaving the vehicle behind. Before leaving it parked for weeks, take it for a quick highway run (to keep the battery charged and circulate fluids), clean out all food and trash, top off the gas, and check campus rules about long-term parking. If storing the vehicle off-campus, use a well-lit, secure lot and remove all valuables and anything else of interest from inside the car. Where possible, avoid parking under trees and use a sunshade in hot climates to protect the interior.

Pro Tip: A fitted car cover can protect the paint from sun damage, dust, pollen, and bird droppings during long-term storage.

LEAVING THE CAR AT HOME?

One of my favorite things to remind our community members to do before school starts each fall is to check with their auto insurance company to see if there is a "student away" or "student pause" program available if the car will be staying home.

Not all insurance carriers offer this, but those that do can provide potentially significant savings on car insurance for students heading off to college. Some plans require the school to be a minimum distance of 100 miles from home, but the student will still be covered when at home during breaks without needing to turn the insurance on and off. There can be additional costs involved in starting and stopping insurance, as well as other potential hassles.

Key Actions to Take

- ☐ **Research campus and city parking rules before deciding to bring a car.**
- ☐ **Pay your housing or enrollment deposit early if it will help you secure parking pass priority.**
- ☐ **Budget for all costs—parking, gas, tickets, maintenance, and insurance.**

- [ ] Establish clear rules for who can drive or ride in the car and specify the distance it can be driven from campus.
- [ ] Stock the trunk with safety and convenience essentials.
- [ ] Encourage responsible, sober driving, and always have a plan for a safe ride home.

20

Packing for College

A Four-Week Plan Ending with How to Pack the Car

What You'll Take Away

- The four-phase Dorm Move-In Plan to help you pack items for each phase together
- A week-by-week plan leading up to leaving for college move-in day
- Smart labeling and packing tricks to make the day easier
- A list of supplies to gather for move-in day
- A strategy for packing the car with a last-in, first-needed approach

While the list and steps in this chapter will be most relevant to those driving to college, those flying will also find helpful ideas and tips for a smooth move-in. Please also see chapter 3 for specific planning and recommendations when flying to college.

PACKING TIMELINE

Packing strategically makes move-in day smoother and less frustrating. You'll have only a small space in which to pile bags and bins and boxes, so the less you have to rummage through everything to find what you need, the better.

This chapter outlines the preparation process starting about four weeks before your college move-in day, all the way through packing the car. (The next chapter provides a detailed plan for move-in day.)

UNDERSTANDING THE FOUR-PHASE DORM MOVE-IN PLAN

Before I get into the packing plan, let's take a quick look at the four-phase Dorm Move-In Plan outlined on page 265, as you'll want to pack by phase as much as possible. Following this plan, from packing through move-in day, will help everything run smoothly.

When you arrive at the dorm room on move-in day, you'll approach the room using these four phases:

PHASE 1: Quickly clean surfaces, rearrange or adjust college-issued furniture, and set up important items.

PHASE 2: Hang the big and high decor and make the bed.
PHASE 3: Unpack, organize, and decorate.
PHASE 4: Set up tech, store large items, document valuables, clean up, and take photos.

These are the items to pack together by phase. Label bags, bins, and boxes with a 1, 2, 3, or 4 accordingly.

Items Needed per Dorm Move-In Plan Phase

Phase 1	**Phase 2**	**Phase 3**	**Phase 4**
Doorstops	Drawer liners	Nightstand	Laptop
Fan	Adhesive for wall decor	Clothes	Monitor
Vacuum and move-in cleaning supplies	Air purifier	Food/appliances/ food storage	TV/TV stand
Fridge	Storage furniture/under-bed storage	Toiletries	Speakers
Mattress encasement and topper	Headboard	Laundry hamper and supplies	Sports equipment
Surge protectors	Mini-kitchen shelving, if using	Desk hutch/ chair/ accessories and school supplies	Musical instruments
Step stool	Microwave	Ottoman	Other
First aid kit	Closet organizers	Other decor	
Toilet paper	Rug		
Tool kit	Curtains		
	Remainder of bedding		

IN THE MONTH BEFORE MOVE-IN DAY

In chapter 4, I discussed setting up a staging area at home for your college purchases (see page 53). If you don't have everything in a staging area yet, please designate a space and gather together everything that is going to college. This does not include personal items used on a daily basis.

Verify Payments and Paperwork

Schools primarily communicate with students, not parents, regarding enrollment and housing deposits, registering for orientation or move-in day time slots, class registration, move-in day procedures, and almost everything else, except information available through the parent portal.

Be sure the student regularly checks their portal, email, and any other communications from the school so they do not miss any time-sensitive information or details about what is needed to check in on move-in day. For example, you may need vaccination records or medical tests. We needed a sickle cell anemia test for my older son (an athlete) and a tuberculosis test for my younger son. Those are not easy to get done at the last minute! You may also need to provide proof of medical insurance or dorm insurance, a student ID, and other relevant information.

Gather Your Moving Bags

Moving bags are the single best invention in recent years for college moves, and if you're not familiar with them, you're about to agree with me wholeheartedly!

Most students will need six to eight moving bags (about 80 liters/ 21 gallons each) for a dorm move. I love the kind with backpack straps, as they make the bags that much easier to carry. Overpackers, especially those who are fashion enthusiasts, will need a few extra bags. If you're moving into an apartment-style dorm with private bathrooms and kitchen space, you'll need more bags for those items.

Gather Other Packing and Move-In Supplies

Packing supplies:

- Painter's tape
- Permanent markers for labeling
- Stretch wrap to secure filled drawer towers

Check Your Dorm Packing Checklist, at Least Twice

It is challenging to keep track of what has been purchased, received, returned, and checked off the list, so now is a good time to review your work and mark off the progress. As you unbox items, place them in the staging area. If you put something in a moving bag, mark it as packed.

Reconfirm Decisions with Your Roommate

Miscommunication happens, and so does remembering everything needed when getting ready for college. If you haven't checked in with your roommate lately, it is worth doing so to ensure that they've been able to narrow down or purchase the items they agreed to share. Give them an update on your progress with the shared items you will be providing.

If you haven't shared what you are buying with each other, do it now while you're still within the return/exchange window.

Unbox and Get Organized

Open the boxes if you haven't already done so. Check for quality, color, feel, parts, size, and functionality. This includes the larger appliances, which can be damaged during shipping. Keep the boxes and packing material for now, along with the receipts. Start organizing items into categories—bedding, storage, furniture, closet, desk, etc. Don't start packing yet; simply group and organize items.

If you think of other items you may need as you unbox something else, add them to your list before you forget. For example, if you open up a shower curtain, you may remember that you still need shower curtain rings or a liner. Write it down now—there is too much to try to keep in your head during this time!

> **Pro Tip:** Keep the shipping boxes for now. It is best to dispose of boxes and packing materials before arriving at the dorm, but you'll need some for transportation, and you might still make a return. Hang on to the small and medium-size boxes for care packages.

Assembly Trial Run

For items that require assembly, consider taking the time to assemble them now. Even if you can't transport the item assembled, do a practice run now. This has two big benefits.

1. You'll know early if any parts are missing or damaged, and have time to remedy this.
2. Having assembled an item before move-in day will cut assembly time and frustration by a good bit when assembling the second time with experience.

Pre-Launder

Wash all bedding and towels, except for the mattress topper, which should remain sealed for transport. Store the clean bedding and towels in zippered storage cubes or bags. Throw in a dryer sheet or two to maintain freshness. You can use these same cubes or bags to store extra linens and off-season clothes in the dorm room.

Pack a Few Bags

Using the phases outlined earlier in the chapter, start putting items from the same phase into the moving bags. As you pack bags, bins, and boxes, label them with the phase number and the contents, and mark them as packed on your dorm packing checklist. Many of the moving bags have a small, clear window on the side that holds an index card—this is a great place to put a list of what is inside.

How to Label Bags

Name

Room #

Phase 3: Desk Accessories, Lamp, Laundry Supplies

For added visual cues, use colorful painter's tape to label each bag with the corresponding phase number.

Ship Ahead

If you plan to ship any items ahead, confirm the address, labeling requirements, and school or recipient policies regarding pre-move-in deliveries.

Return Unnecessary Items

If you've purchased items that you know won't be used, return them as soon as possible. The next few weeks will be a flurry of activity, and you may not have the time or energy to tackle returns once you're back from college drop-off.

THE WEEK BEFORE MOVE-IN DAY

Continue updating the dorm packing checklist, unboxing, and packing while using the labeling method outlined above.

Clothes

Start gathering the clothes that will be moving to college and consider the following (the night before move-in is not the time to worry about any of these things):

- Does anything need to be washed or dry-cleaned before it goes?
- Do dress shoes need to be cleaned up or polished?
- Do sets have all their pieces, such as the belt for a belted dress?
- Do all socks have their mate?
- Are there off-season items that can be left at home for now and swapped out during a visit home or a Parents' Weekend?

Keep hanging clothes on their hangers, or move them to the hangers that will be used in the dorm. When you're ready to pack the clothes for the move, place them in the moving bag, as pictured below, or in a heavy-duty garbage bag if you aren't using moving bags.

Unloading hanging clothes is the easiest when they are already on hangers!

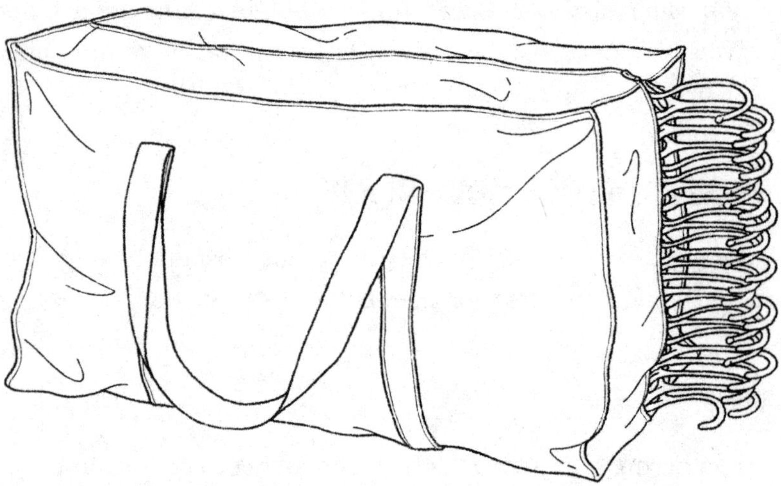

Use a moving bag and keep hanging clothes on hangers when moving—it is so easy to unzip the bag and hang the clothes right in the closet when you arrive in the dorm room!

If you're bringing drawers, pack them with clothes and any other items that need a home for travel. To secure the drawers for carrying, wrap them closed with stretch wrap. Be careful not to overpack the plastic drawer towers.

Cleaning and Packing Prep

- Put any potentially leaky or open items into ziplock bags.
- Keep move-in day cleaning supplies separate and in the move-in day bag.
- Open the air purifier to ensure that there is no packaging on the filter.
- Open any other appliances, clean interior parts, run a full cleaning cycle (e.g., for a coffee maker), etc.
- Clean new water pitchers and food storage containers.
- Clean new dishes, cups, and silverware.

Allow all of the above to dry completely before packing them.

Pack-the-Car Trial Run

This is not necessary, but if there is concern about fitting everything in the car, some like to do a trial run to be sure it all fits. If you have a mini fridge, it is best to move it in an upright position.

Ship-Ahead Details

If you shipped ahead to the school or elsewhere, be sure you know where pickup is and how it is handled. Be prepared for long lines, and allow time for this in your schedule.

Shared Notes

Get familiar with the Notes app on your phone and, even better, how to collaborate on one note with the whole family. Have a note ready during move-in to jot down any quick shopping needs or errands to do after move-in as you put the room together. Things will come up that were overlooked or surprises, and it will help to write these down as you go.

Plan for Move-In Day Food, Drink, and Other Items

Pick up snacks, water, and any other essentials you need for your trip. For that feeling you'll have in the car on the way to college, consider antacids, ginger ale, or something else that will settle your stomach!

> **Pro Tip:** Gather some old washcloths, wet them, roll them up, and stick them in a freezer baggie. These will go in your move-in day cooler. Use them initially as ice packs to keep drinks cold and later to cool off and clean your hands.

THE DAY BEFORE MOVE-IN DAY (OR THE DAY BEFORE TRAVEL DAY)

Finish Packing

Finish packing all the dorm essentials and clothes. Start early on the clothes—they always seem to take longer than expected and cause angst due to overpacking.

Double-check your list. Is there anything on the list that does not indicate that it has been packed?

To Do's to Make Tomorrow Easier

- Be sure to plan what you will wear on move-in day and set it aside so that it doesn't get packed. Definitely wear comfortable closed-toe shoes or sneakers, so you can wear socks, too.
- Pack snacks or even lunch if it's going to be a long day. You don't need anyone getting hangry on top of all the emotions! Parking and navigating around campus may be challenging, and campus restaurant outlets may not be open. Therefore, bring what you'll need and avoid relying on eating out or picking up food.
- If you're driving, prep a cooler with lots of water—more than you think you'll need. Did you freeze those washcloths? Don't forget those tomorrow. Put a sticky note on the cooler to remind you.
- For most of the country, it will be hot on move-in day. Start hydrating today—don't wait until tomorrow.
- If you're making a day trip, pack a change of clothes and toiletries to freshen up for dinner after move-in or for the ride home. (Put these in a small bag that you can keep separate from all the dorm gear.) Consider those post-move-in photos in the new dorm setup, too.
- Assemble a small first aid kit for move-in day, including Band-Aids, antibiotic ointment, and ibuprofen.
- Pack as much as you can into the car today/tonight (see the order on page 255).

Have the Family Discussions

Now is a good time to get everyone on the same page for tomorrow.

- Have dinner together as a family. Water glasses all around, hydrating early!

- Remind the student that this is their time, that you're there to help with the move but the decisions are theirs.
- It is their time, except for the pictures. These are nonnegotiable, and you don't want to argue about them tomorrow. Just ask them to agree to photos as requested to help make the day enjoyable.
- Reconfirm your guidance about staying safe, making good decisions, not taking any pills (they might be laced with something), treading lightly with parties and partying, never walking alone, practicing safe sex—whatever you feel you need to reiterate. Better to do this now than tomorrow while you're anxiously on the road, busy unpacking, or saying goodbye.
- Hopefully, you've already had conversations about spending money and who is paying for what; if not, have those conversations now, too. Don't forget to discuss expenses such as gas, restaurant meals, dates, haircuts, toiletries, party outfits, makeup, manicures, etc.
- Agree on communication for the days and weeks after move-in. If the student prefers text over FaceTime, let them guide the method. Just ask for regular check-ins so you know they're okay.
- Encourage them to proactively seek any needed guidance, whether it be academic, financial, physical, spiritual, or mental health–related. Encourage them to get off to a good start and not be afraid to ask for help—it is absolutely acceptable!
- Agree to leave a little earlier tomorrow to help reduce stress, especially if you have a specific move-in time. Allow for a little traffic, locating your check-in location, and finding parking.

Pro Tip: Be sure to get the mailing address for the student at school. Store it in your phone in case you need to ship a few things after your drive home. Also send it to grandparents or anyone else who may want to send notes, care packages, or small gifts to the new college student.

HOW TO PACK THE CAR FOR MOVE-IN DAY

If you're driving to the airport to fly to college, the order for packing the car is whatever is easiest for you to unload at the airport!

If you're driving to school, there are three possible move-in arrival scenarios to consider before packing the car for move-in day. In each scenario, you'll want to label each item with a phase (1 through 4)—see the chart on page 244.

Scenario	Car Packing Plan
Park in a parking area near the dorm building and unload the car from there. No immediate limit to the amount of time you're allowed to park.	Clearly label each item with a phase (1 through 4) and the student's name and room number. Pack items in the car in the reverse order that they will be needed when you arrive at the dorm.
Pull up to a designated unloading zone and unload everything onto the curb or into a bin yourself. Immediately move the car to a designated parking area.	Clearly label each item with a phase (1 through 4) and the student's name and room number. If multiple people will help unload the car, be sure to pack all phase 1 items last so that the first person out of the car can take those and get started while others unload and move the car.
Pull up to a designated unloading zone, and some very helpful volunteers will unload your car and carry everything directly to the dorm room!	Clearly label each item with a phase (1 through 4) and the student's name and room number. Consider bringing some \$5 or \$10 gift cards to thank the volunteers who help you move everything.

These are general guidelines. Of course, your Tetris skills may need to win out over the perfect order to make it all fit!

One important note is to keep the mini fridge upright during transportation, even if you have to take it out of the box to help it fit in the car. If you must lay it down, please stand it up when you arrive in the dorm room, but do not plug it in yet. Wait at least the amount of time it was lying down or, better yet, twenty-four hours to allow the fluids to drain back to their correct position.

With everything labeled and packed in the Dorm Move-In Plan order, you're ready for the big day. In the next chapter, I'll take you through the step-by-step Dorm Move-In Plan from arrival through photos. I'll leave the saying goodbye part to you!

Key Actions to Take

- ☐ **Establish a dorm gear staging area in your home.**
- ☐ **Determine whether to fly or drive to move-in day.**
- ☐ **Make any necessary hotel or car rental arrangements well in advance.**
- ☐ **Research how move-in day is handled, including how dates and times are assigned and if there are helpers at the dorms.**
- ☐ **Double-check for necessary documentation and IDs before leaving home.**

21

It's Move-In Day

Be Ready with This Four-Phase Plan

What You'll Take Away

- **How to prepare ahead to make move-in day smooth**
- **The tools and supplies to bring**
- **My perfected four-phase step-by-step plan to keep the day running smoothly**
- **Tips for the goodbyes when it is time to go**

My goal for this entire chapter—and, in fact, for this entire book—is to help you have a smooth move-in day without any surprises or hiccups. It is already an emotional day for everyone involved, so the more prepared and confident you feel walking into the room, the more I hope you'll be able to enjoy this milestone day.

Please know this: Even with all the planning and preparation, there will be some minor blips. You'll see social media photos that make you think everyone has a storybook move-in day, but I promise it wasn't perfect. It will be hot, emotional, crowded, and occasionally frantic. Things will break in transit, the room layout or dimensions will differ from what was provided, furniture won't fit, parts will be missing, and tempers will flare. There will be a few poignant moments and some straight out of *The Exorcist*. And all of this is normal; everyone handles stress and emotions differently. Just be prepared, whether you are the parent or the student, to give some grace and take deep breaths. Smiles and hugs help, and a good laugh fixes just about anything.

EARLY PLANNING FOR MOVE-IN DAY

I've sprinkled some of these steps into previous chapters because planning ahead is important for many of these, but this is the complete list of things to do as early as possible, in case you've skipped right to this chapter.

Travel and Logistics

Busy periods, such as college move-in, often result in higher airfares and more expensive hotel rooms. Make arrangements as early as possible.

- **Decide who is going with you.** This is a tough decision. You want to bring the younger sibling, but there really won't be room in the car, and the dorm room is already going to be crowded. If other relatives need to come, limit their time in the dorm room to facilitate a smooth move-in process. Check with the school to see if there is a limit on the number of guests or helpers.

- **Book air travel.** If you have some time before your trip, set up airfare price trackers to be alerted when prices drop. But book well in advance, especially if you're headed into a smaller market. Consider airlines with lower baggage fees.
- **Look into shipping ahead.** Some schools will start accepting packages for you a week or even a month in advance. If you're flying to college, this can be a big help. If the school does not hold packages, check to see if your hotel will hold shipments for you or ask a friend or family member who lives close to the college.
- **Book a hotel room/lodging.** If you need a hotel room and haven't made a reservation yet, do so ASAP. Some schools offer hotel recommendations and discounted rates. Check your college's website for this information. Alternatively, check Airbnb listings in the city and their availability—you might appreciate having access to a washer and dryer after a long trip or for a longer stay. In small and medium-size towns, hotel reservations get more expensive the closer you get to move-in time. The same is true for Parents' Weekend, home football games, move-out, and graduation—always book as far in advance as possible, and consider a refundable rate to give yourself flexibility.
- **Make dinner reservations.** If you will be in town the night before move-in or staying the night of, consider making dinner reservations now to ensure that you'll have an option after a long day of moving. Small towns will be overrun with families looking for dinner spots.

School Move-In Process

Check with your school to understand the move-in day process, which may include:

- **Move-In Time Slots:** Some schools are more flexible, but many require you to sign up for a specific time slot. This will be your time to unload and bring your belongings to your room. You will likely need to move the car immediately after unloading, so decide who will move it ahead of time and know where it needs to be parked. I recommend an early-in-the-day move-in time if that works with your schedule and if there is availability.
- **A Check-In Location:** Do you need to start at a central check-in point before arriving at the dorm building? Do you need to bring specific identification, special paperwork, proof of payments, or medical records with you for check-in?
- **Scheduled Freshman Activities:** On move-in day, there may be late-afternoon or evening orientation activities. Additionally, athletes and band members may need to report for practice or a meeting, or Greek recruitment activities may get under way. These are all good reasons to schedule a morning move-in time slot so you have time to get things done and say goodbye before the student needs to head out.
- **Time Limits:** Is there a specific time limit on how long family helpers may stay to unpack and set up the room? Some people confuse the move-in time slot with the total time you can be there, but typically, the move-in time slot is just the timeframe during which your car can be in the unloading zone. Please confirm that this is the case.
- **Large Rolling Carts:** The school may provide large carts for

moving items from your car to your room. These are big enough to fit most of what you have in the car in one trip. There may be wait times for carts and elevators, so pack your patience.

- **Move-In Helpers:** The school may provide volunteers to unload your car and bring your things to your room. This is a fantastic service if it is available. Consider bringing a few $5 or $10 gift cards from local spots to give as a token of appreciation.
- **Elevators:** Know that elevators will be in high demand and may have long wait times, so you may decide to take the stairs more than you'd planned rather than wait for an elevator. At a minimum, expect one person to ride with the cart in the elevator and the others to take the stairs with light loads. Pack (and dress) accordingly!
- **Student Parking:** For students bringing a car to campus, be sure to know the rules in advance, in case you need to apply for a parking permit or park in a designated freshman lot. While parking enforcement may look the other way on move-in day, they will probably not be lenient for long!

THE MOVE-IN TOOL KIT

This may seem like a long list, but it is better to be prepared than to be stuck in a building far from your car or a store while trying to finish a project. If possible, bring extras that will help fellow families in the hall who may not be as prepared as you are. Helping other families in their tense moments or just as an act of kindness is always appreciated and an excellent way for students to meet, too!

As for the cleaning supplies, yes, the dorm room should be

clean. Is it always? Absolutely not, at least not up to most of our standards. Have the supplies with you and do a quick fifteen-minute clean if needed before you start moving in your items.

Tools and Supplies

- Painter's tape to tape rug corners or for other needs
- Plastic cup to hold furniture parts during assembly
- Rubbing alcohol to clean walls for adhesive hangers
- Rubber mallet, for adjusting bed slats (if beds are adjustable) and securing assembled furniture
- Heavy wedge doorstop—especially helpful as most doors have auto-close mechanisms. Grab a few so that you can share them with others in the hall who didn't know to bring one. After move-in day, use doorstops to prop the door open when you're feeling social to invite your hallmates to stop in.
- Nonadhesive drawer liners (optional, but nice to have for the dresser and desk drawers)
- Scissors
- Tape measure
- Pencil
- Level, for hanging wall art
- Permanent marker, for labeling cords, chargers, and other items
- Small toolbox. Tools are always needed. In lieu of a toolbox, bring Phillips-head and standard screwdrivers, pliers, an Allen wrench, a standard wrench, and a measuring tape.
- Stepladder, for reaching high wall decor, top closet shelves, and curtains
- WD-40. Doors and drawers tend to be squeaky!

- Zip ties. Bring a variety of sizes and strengths to handle different situations.
- Small move-in day first aid bag. Include Band-Aids, antibiotic ointment, and ibuprofen.
- Trash bags. Have a few larger ones for packing materials, and leave behind a box of kitchen garbage bags for the student's kitchen-size dorm room trash can (they will need the big size!).
- If there's rain in the forecast, bring large yard waste trash bags or small tarps to help loose items (e.g., a TV that is already out of the box) stay dry while they're being transported from the car to the dorm.
- If the school does not provide carts or helpers, a cart for heavy or bulky items will be helpful, especially if there is an elevator.

Cleaning Supplies

- Disinfecting wipes
- Paper towels
- Multipurpose cleaner
- Bathroom cleaning supplies and disposable gloves (if the student has a private or semi-private bathroom)
- Vacuum cleaner/mop

For the Student and Family Helpers

- Cooler with plenty of water and cold washcloths
- Snacks that are easy to eat without plates or silverware (use paper towels for napkins)
- Toilet paper (if the student has a private or semi-private bathroom) and tissues

- Hand sanitizer or hand soap
- Change of clothes for after the move when unpacking is complete

What to Wear on Move-In Day

You might be wondering why I'm covering this—shouldn't it be obvious?

Comfortable, breathable clothes are important, but also keep in mind that there is a lot of leaning over, bending down, reaching up, and climbing ladders. Wear shirts long enough to cover your midsection while you're bending and stretching, and skip the skirts and sundresses.

Wear sneakers for stability when carrying, hauling, and climbing ladders. Save the flip-flops or slides for after move-in is complete.

HOW LONG DOES MOVE-IN TAKE?

I'm often asked how long to allow to complete the move-in and setup of a dorm room. For a basic room with minimal wall decor or furniture assembly, you should be able to complete it in a couple of hours. If a roommate is also moving in, it will slow you down a bit as you work around their move-in crew.

For students with a lot of decor, clothes, full bathrooms, and roommate-coordinated bedding and furniture, I've seen some move-ins go into a second day.

While you're planning your day and considering timeframes, please do the following to factor in these variables:

- **Pad the schedule.** Allow extra time for traffic, construction, or simply navigating this new area.

- **Be prepared for weather.** Keep an eye on the forecast, as rain can make move-in day quite challenging. If rain is forecasted, have raincoats, umbrellas, a couple of old towels, and a few tarps available for moving. Expect weather-related delays and schedule adjustments. Bringing a complete change of clothes, including shoes, is a good idea.
- **Leave time for shopping.** Set aside an hour or two after unpacking to run to big-box stores or a hardware store for any missing items. Keep in mind that most will be quite picked over. A quick grocery run to stock the fridge or a trip to the college bookstore for swag is always appreciated, too.

Pro Tip: Make a good impression from the onset with good hallway etiquette. Don't take up the whole hallway, keep the volume down, and return carts promptly. Be helpful and courteous, and greet others with a smile.

THE FOUR-PHASE DORM MOVE-IN PLAN

Before you put anything in the room, *take a picture* of how you found the dorm room on arrival. Take a few if you can't see the whole room from the doorway. You'll be thankful for the before pics later.

If you have to bring everything to the room right away (or if it is delivered there), can you use a little hallway space to move the later-phase items out of the way for a bit? Labeled bins and bags are helpful for staying organized, finding what you need quickly, and eliminating the need to dig through bags.

If you're using moving bags, as you empty them, flatten and fold them as best you can, and put them all inside one still-open bag.

Pro Tip: Printable PDFs with checklists for each phase are available on TheDormGuide.com.

Phase 1: Do a Light Cleaning and Prep Important Items

Below are the items and aspects of the room that need to be dealt with right away. Before you begin, wipe down surfaces, including the desk, chair, bed rails, dresser, insides of drawers, and rod and shelves inside the closet. Run the vacuum around the entire room, and if the floor is a solid surface, determine whether it needs to be mopped. If there is a private or semi-private bathroom that roommates have not used yet, give it a thorough cleaning. If you rented a MicroFridge, give it an interior and exterior clean as well.

1. **Fan:** Plug in the fan and get it going in the room. It may feel cool now, but once multiple people are moving around and working, it will get warm.
2. **Mattress Encasement:** Clean off the mattress with a disinfecting wipe and let it dry (the fan should help). If you brought a mattress encasement, put it around the mattress and zip it closed.
3. **Mattress Topper:** Open the mattress topper and let it expand on top of the mattress. The instructions may say it needs twenty-four to forty-eight hours to fully expand, but give it several hours today without sitting or lying on it, and it will be fine. You may have to move it later to hang wall art, and that's okay. I've tested many mattress toppers over the years, and they all expand within six hours.
4. **Surge Protectors:** Bring out the surge protectors and locate the outlets on your side of the room.

5. **Layout:** Finalize the placement of school-provided furniture. If students want to explore different options, now is the time! Move furniture around (if allowed) to achieve the desired layout. Consider the outlet locations for the desk, mini-kitchen setup, and TV (if applicable).
6. **Bed Height:** Adjust the bed height to your preferred level. This is easier with two people. Not all beds are adjustable, and even if they are, some schools do not let you adjust the height yourself. Be sure to account for under-bed storage, and if you can adjust the height of the bed, use the rubber mallet to gently knock each leg support out of its current position and place it firmly in the new position.
7. **Mini Fridge:** Unpack and plug in the fridge. Important note: If you had to lay the fridge on its side for transport, do not plug it in yet. It must stand upright for at least as long as it was lying down, if not for a full twenty-four hours, to allow the fluids in the coils to return to their proper location. And a reminder to never plug a mini fridge or microwave into an extension cord. These should only be plugged directly into the wall (ideally) or into a sturdy surge protector. Mini fridges also need to vent out the back and should never be placed in a closed cabinet.

For more information on all the items in Phase 1, please see the following pages:

Fans—page 215

Mattress encasements and toppers—page 91

Surge protectors—page 162

Bed height—page 83

Mini fridges—page 149

Do not put the rug down yet, in case you need to move furniture around to hang items.

Grab some water, take it all in, and move on to Phase 2. Take a pic of your work in progress if you want to chronicle the day, not just the before-and-after.

Phase 2: Hang High Decor and Set Up the Big Stuff

This phase is the bulk of the work, assembly, and heavy lifting.

1. **Wall Decor If Using Adhesives, Part 1**: Be sure you know the dorm rules for hanging things on the walls long before you arrive for move-in; tacks and nails are typically permitted only with Sheetrock. If you are required to use adhesives, determine where you plan to hang any wall decor or curtains, and use rubbing alcohol to clean those areas. Allow it to dry, then follow the package instructions exactly to hang the hooks, strips, and curtain rod holders. When it says to wait one hour before using, please heed this recommendation! The adhesive needs to cure for at least this long. (Leave replacement strips behind in case replacements are needed.)
2. **Wall Decor If Using Tacks or Nails:** Hang all wall decor items now. These may include flags, framed art, posters, string lights, neon signs, and names/letters.
3. **Air Purifier:** Plug in the air purifier if you brought one. Try to place it near the air vent, off the floor, and away from room corners, if possible. Ensure that there is no plastic wrap around the filter inside.
4. **Furniture Assembly:** Put together any furniture items. Have someone do this in a common area outside the room if that's allowed. Bring a small plastic cup or bowl to keep hardware from being misplaced.

5. **Under-Bed Storage:** Place storage under the bed.
6. **Headboard:** If you have a headboard with legs, install it now. You'll need long, heavy-duty zip ties to connect the headboard legs to the bed frame. Use several to maximize stability, and utilize the horizontal slats by placing the zip ties strategically just above them. The headboard legs will not touch the floor, and they may be adjustable on the back of the headboard if you need longer legs for more stability. Refer to page 175 for more information on attaching headboards to dorm beds.
7. **Closet:** Install closet organizers such as hanging racks, shoe racks, double hanging rods, bins, and baskets.
8. **Drawers:** Install nonadhesive drawer liners if you're using them. You'll need scissors to cut them to size.
9. **Rug:** Vacuum the area where the rug will go and pick up any debris from the moving and unpacking so far. Unroll the rug in place and tape the corners down if necessary to prevent tripping.
10. **Kitchen:** Set up the kitchen area. Place the fridge in the desired spot, then add racks, shelves, or other mini-kitchen structures around it. Place the microwave in its place if it is separate.
11. **Desk:** If you brought a desk hutch, place it on top of the desk. You should not need to secure it, but you can use Velcro strips, adhesive strips, or putty to add a little stability, if desired.
12. **Bed:** Make the bed with all the layers, throw blankets, and pillows.

For more information on all the items in Phase 2, please see the following pages:

Decor—page 219

Air purifiers—page 212

Furniture—page 171

Under-bed storage—page 114

Headboards—page 174

Closet organization—page 131

Rugs—page 224

Kitchen—page 146

Desk—page 135

Bedding—page 90

Take a water break, have a quick snack, and snap a few photos of your progress.

Some students decide that once the big things are in the room, they want to do the rest themselves. This is relatively common, so please don't take it personally.

Phase 3: Unpack

If you haven't yet, it is time to bring in the last of the items from the car and start the unpacking, organizing, and decorating phase.

If your roommate is also unpacking, try to work in different parts of the room so you don't step on each other's toes.

1. **Nightstand:** If you're using a nightstand or a shelf, install it next to the bed.
2. **Clothes, Shoes, and Accessories:** Unload clothes into the closet and drawers. If there are space issues, consider storing off-

season clothes and shoes in a moving bag behind the under-bed storage.

3. **Appliances and Food Storage:** Set up any appliances and food storage.
4. **Toiletries:** Find a home for toiletries and place a boot tray or another mat to hold wet items.
5. **Desk:** Organize desk accessories and school supplies.
6. **Vanity Area:** Utilize organizers and drawers to create a functional vanity space, likely at the desk if there is no sink or mirror in the room.
7. **Laundry and Cleaning:** Place the laundry hamper in its designated spot, and find somewhere to store laundry and cleaning supplies.
8. **Extra Linens:** Store extra bedding and towels.
9. **Tabletop Decor:** Set up lamps, clocks, charging stations, and other tabletop decor and devices.
10. **Curtains:** If you're using adhesive hooks and the required curing time has passed, install the curtains now. If you're using a tension rod, you can install the curtains at any time. Consider using painter's tape on the wall before installing the tension rod over it to prevent paint from peeling.
11. **Wall Decor If Using Adhesives, Part 2:** If you're using adhesive products that need to cure, and it has been at least an hour since you put up the hook/strip, you can go ahead and hang your decor on them now.
12. **Ottoman:** If you've been keeping the ottoman out of the way, now is the time to place it by the bed or in an appropriate spot.

Phase 4: Set Up Technology, Document Valuables, and Do a Final Cleanup

Save the tech setup for last. There could be technical issues, and you don't want to hold up everything else because you can't get a gaming device or TV connected to the Wi-Fi. That can be solved later.

1. **Laptop:** Plug the laptop into a surge protector and secure the power cord so it stays on the desk when the laptop is removed.
2. **Monitor:** If you use a computer monitor, find a suitable spot for it on the desk, ideally near the back and under the desk hutch, if you have one.
3. **TV/TV Stand:** TVs typically sit on a dresser, the top of a desk hutch, or a mobile TV cart.
4. **Smart Tech:** Unless there is a Bluetooth connection, you will likely be unable to connect to smart products, as campus network settings do not allow third-party devices to log in and connect to them.
5. **Sports Equipment:** If you're bringing larger sports equipment to the dorm room, you may need to use the space behind the under-bed storage to store it. This is especially true for large items such as golf clubs.
6. **Musical Instruments:** Each year I am asked where to store and display a guitar. Most hope it can be stored on a wall hook. Unfortunately, without the ability to screw into the wall, a wall hook will not be possible. A floor stand may be the best option.

Document Your Valuables

Once the tech setup is complete, take pictures of the valuable items in the room, including close-ups of their serial numbers.

Also include other valuable non-tech items, such as jewelry, golf clubs, a bike, furniture, and appliances.

If you're storing items in a safe with a key, take a picture of the key so that you'll know what you're looking for when it goes missing. If you're using a combination lock, set it up and store the combination in a shared note on the phone.

Store these photos in the cloud or in a shared album with parents. Hopefully, you will not need to reference the album again, but it is helpful to have pictures of these items in your dorm room in case they are ever required for a claim or as proof of ownership.

Do a Quick Cleanup

Once everything is in place, find somewhere to store the empty bags and bins that are staying in the dorm room, and take the collected move-in trash to the trash chute or dumpster.

Leave at least two of the folded-up moving bags with the student. These are great for visits home, laundry, beach trips, tailgating, and more. They will definitely come in handy.

If needed, do a final pass with the vacuum cleaner and the Swiffer mop to take care of move-in messes.

Photo Op!

The time has come to take some "after" shots of the fully assembled dorm room. Try to get some from the same angle as your "before" shots to show the best comparisons!

Take some photos of the student alone in their room, with the roommate(s) if they are around, and with the family. I recommend full-family photos and separate photos of the student with each family member. Hopefully, your roommate is nearby, or you've met people in the hall during the day who can help take your family photos.

If you're planning to post photos to social media, ensure that everyone in the photos consents and that the roommate is okay with having their side of the room on social media.

MISSION ACCOMPLISHED!

It's hard to believe that after months of applications, decisions, and shopping lists, this day has finally arrived. Move-in is done, and a new chapter officially begins.

If you don't have plans for lunch, dinner, or a grocery run afterward, here's a word of advice: Don't linger. This is the student's time to meet hallmates, lend a hand to others still unpacking, and begin settling into campus life.

Double-check that everyone has their own car keys, snap a few last photos, and say your goodbyes. Give yourself credit for how well you've prepared your student, and trust that they are ready to take it from here.

It's time to let them step fully into this adventure, and for you to exhale. You did it.

Key Actions to Take

- ☐ **Make travel arrangements as early as possible, including booking flights, hotel rooms, and car rentals.**
- ☐ **Confirm your move-in time, helpers/visitors, school process, and parking permit.**
- ☐ **Assemble your move-in tool kit.**
- ☐ **Print or bookmark the four-phase Dorm Move-In Plan.**
- ☐ **Assign tasks to helpers (moving the car, assembling furniture, cleaning).**

22

Common Dorm Room Challenges & Recommended Fixes

What You'll Take Away

- **The most common dorm room problems students face after move-in**
- **How to handle problems calmly and confidently**
- **Gentle coaching suggestions to let the student take the lead in resolving issues**

Move-in day might feel like the finish line, but it's really just the beginning. Once the boxes are unpacked and the parents head home, students quickly face the new reality that they're officially on their own. New challenges appear almost daily, and adulting sets in faster than expected. Combine these emotions with some loneliness or homesickness, and it can feel overwhelming.

Whether the roommate is snoring, you're missing the comfort of home, or you have sudden, unexplained skin breakouts, there is a lot to manage. The good news? Most of these challenges are normal, temporary, and fixable.

This chapter covers some of the most common post-move-in challenges and recommended solutions for each.

ROOMMATE & SUITEMATE CHALLENGES

Challenge: General Roommate Conflicts

Roommate issues are one of the most common complaints after move-in. Different sleep schedules, cleanliness levels, personal hygiene habits, or social activities can strain even good matches.

Recommended Fix

Encourage students to have a few brief "roommate check-in" meetings early on, whether things are going well or not. They should calmly discuss expectations for quiet hours, cleaning, and guests. If issues are discussed but don't improve, RAs are trained mediators who can help prevent escalation.

> **Pro Tip:** Encourage students to schedule a short weekly check-in with their roommate for the first month; even just five minutes can prevent months of tension. If a face-to-face conversation is uncomfortable, have a brief text message exchange. "Hi, [Roommate Name]—just checking in on how things are working for you in our dorm room. Anything I can do a little differently to make life easier for you?"

Challenge: Roommate Not Cleaning Up After Themself

Unwashed dishes, overflowing trash, and piles of dirty laundry can quickly breed resentment, and sometimes even attract insects.

Recommended Fix

If the roommate's belongings encroach on your side of the room, kindly ask them to respect your personal space. Suggest a cleanup schedule or a simple "Sunday room reset" to spend ten minutes putting misplaced items away and cleaning up any food, dishes, spills, or other unsanitary situations. If the roommate refuses, document the situation and escalate it to the RA if it affects health or livability.

Challenge: Roommate Pushing the Snooze Button for Hours

Few things are more frustrating than an alarm that is continually snoozed while the owner does not get up or turn it off completely.

Recommended Fix

Bring this up in a calm conversation later in the day, not in the heat of the moment. "Your alarm going off every ten minutes in the morning is affecting my sleep. Could you use a watch vibration alarm instead?" If the issue persists, please speak with your RA for further guidance.

Challenge: Difficult Neighbors or Suitemates

If you're in a suite-style or apartment-style dorm room, you likely have multiple people sharing common spaces. The probability of experiencing issues is higher.

Recommended Fix

With multiple roommates and shared spaces that likely include kitchens and bathrooms, a clear roommate agreement is essential. If that didn't happen before move-in, work with your RA to put one in place now. Kind but direct conversations can be helpful, but it can be challenging to stand your ground when multiple personalities are involved.

Challenge: Roommate's Hygiene Habits Affect Shared Space

This is awkward, for sure, and it does happen. Lack of showering or the use of personal hygiene products can quickly make a small space unpleasant.

Recommended Fix

Address the problem kindly but directly: "Hey, the room's been smelling off lately—can we agree to some changes to freshen the air?" If it continues without change, the student should speak to their RA; they are trained to help manage this.

Challenge: Shower/Bathroom Timing Conflicts

I've seen this frequently. Four students share one bathroom, and there is always someone in the shower when you need to use it.

Recommended Fix

The easiest solution is for the roommates to gather together to create a bathroom schedule that works for everyone. You may need to take turns getting up a little earlier to use the shower before class, but if you know this ahead of time, it makes a huge difference. After the schedule is in place, plan a check-in a few weeks later to see how it is working for everyone. Be sure to let the group know if anything changes with your schedule and frees up peak time that you no longer need.

DORM ROOM ISSUES

Challenge: Room Too Hot or Too Cold

Dorm thermostats often have little to no individual control, and older buildings and HVAC systems rarely maintain a comfortable temperature in every room.

Recommended Fix

For hot rooms, 100 percent cotton bedding will be much cooler than microfiber. Layer bedding: Swap out a heavier comforter for a thinner quilt during hot weather. Fans and blackout curtains can also help keep things cool, while a dehumidifier can remove sticky moisture from the air.

In cold rooms, since space heaters and electric blankets are often prohibited, plan to dress in layers and bring plenty of extra bedding. Draft stoppers at the window base or hallway door can keep drafts to a minimum. Report ongoing issues or extreme cases to maintenance; many campuses can manually adjust air output or provide an alternative solution.

Challenge: Mattress Topper Sliding Around

Mattress toppers often shift on slick dorm mattresses during the night. This is exacerbated by loose-fitting bedding on top.

Recommended Fix

A fully elasticized mattress pad and fitted sheet around both the topper and mattress are essential bed layers. You can also add a non-slip grippy rug pad between the mattress and mattress topper, or use corner bedsheet clips to hold everything in place.

Challenge: Pillows Falling off the Bed

Small beds raised up higher than normal mean that when pillows fall off, they go a long way down.

Recommended Fix

Pool noodles zip-tied to the side of the bed frame against the wall will keep the pillows from falling through a small gap. A headboard, a wedge pillow, or a headboard pillow behind the primary pillow will help keep that pillow from falling off the head of the bed. For frequent pillow falls, a bed rail along the side can also be helpful.

Challenge: Wall Art Won't Stay Up

Dorm walls are notoriously resistant to adhesives, especially if the walls are textured or cinder block surfaces with years of grime and layers of paint.

Recommended Fix

Try using outdoor adhesive strips (formulated for temperature and humidity changes) or lightweight poster putty for small prints. When adhesives won't hold, place a strip of painter's tape on the wall, and then apply hot glue for a great hold. You can also put painter's tape on the object you're hanging to protect it from the glue.

Challenge: Poor Study Environment

It's hard to focus when your desk is next to a TV or your roommate's friends are hanging out.

Recommended Fix

If your headphones won't drown out the TV, or your roommate won't take the party elsewhere, the good news is that there are lots of great places to study on a college campus. Scope out quiet areas on campus in addition to study rooms in your dorm and nearby buildings, and, of course, the library. Many college libraries these days have reservable group study rooms where students can work on projects or study for exams together. There are numerous options on campus, so if the dorm room is distracting, find other comfortable and quiet alternatives.

DORM HALL ISSUES

Challenge: Too Much Noise (and Too Little Sleep)

Dorm hallways can be noisy—characterized by linoleum or thin-carpeted floors with little sound absorption, loud students at all hours, music, gatherings, and slamming doors. Noise complaints rise sharply after move-in week, once students have settled in and are socializing.

Recommended Fix

Fans, earplugs, and white noise apps go a long way. Try turning the air purifier on high overnight. If there is a significant gap under the door, roll up a towel or blanket, or buy a door draft stopper. Speak to the RA if the problem becomes chronic, and if it still doesn't improve and significantly impacts sleep, escalate the concern to housing and inquire about moving to a designated quiet floor.

Challenge: Communal Bathroom Issues

From long wait times to zero sink space to questionable cleaning standards, communal bathrooms are often high on the list of issues.

Recommended Fix

To avoid long wait times, try to take advantage of nonpeak hours or get up a little earlier to ensure that you get a shower before your schedule is put at risk.

For sink space, see if there are wall hooks between sinks for a hanging toiletry caddy. If not, use a suction cup hook on the wall or the mirror to hold your items while you use the sink. Lack of cleanliness is a common complaint. The best advice is to use the showers immediately after the cleaning crew has finished their work. Shower shoes are an absolute must. If lack of cleanliness is an ongoing issue, students should politely report it to the housing office.

Challenge: Hair and Skin Issues

Poor dorm water quality, lack of sleep, flawed laundry habits, and dietary changes can trigger unexpected breakouts and new hair issues.

Recommended Fix

Many dorms have hard water, and, as mentioned in chapter 15, students often want to replace showerheads with those that better filter the water. This is not the first year that this has been a problem in the dorm, so discuss options with the RA or the housing office.

Hard water, infrequent washing of bedding, and dietary changes can disrupt skin and hair. Change your pillowcases frequently, drink more water, and make healthier food choices. Try using a clarifying shampoo, and always make time to clean your face and hands before heading to bed.

Challenge: Wet Shower Caddies and Other Items

Students return to their rooms with wet shower caddies or come in from the rain with wet umbrellas, shoes, and backpacks, with nowhere to put them to dry.

Recommended Fix

Don't use a clean towel on the floor for this solution! Clean towels are worth their weight in gold. Designate a spot in the room, even under the bed if that's the only available space, for a rubber boot tray or a dish-drying mat. Regularly clean and dry the shower caddy to prevent mold and mildew, and shake off the umbrella as much as possible before entering the dorm building.

Challenge: Mold or Air-Quality Issues

Older dorms often have inefficient air handling systems with poor ventilation (and temperature control). These issues can lead to excess moisture, which ultimately may result in mold formation.

Recommended Fix

If you notice any visible mold or mildew, please report it immediately. Keep vents clear, and limit shower steam in the dorm room as much as possible. Review chapter 17 for detailed recommendations, including the use of air purifiers or dehumidifiers, if permitted. If the problem persists, insist that the housing department test the air vents for mold and provide commercial-grade appliances to help resolve the issue.

Challenge: Laundry Issues

Soap residue on clothes, clothes that don't seem "clean," and items damaged or missing are common complaints.

Recommended Fix

Colleges use commercial washers and dryers in campus dorm facilities. Compared with the machines you're used to at home, these have fewer settings, smaller drums, and water that doesn't get as hot, so you'll need to shift your laundry habits and expectations. Smaller loads are always recommended, even though that's inconvenient for students who wait weeks to do laundry. Liquid detergent reduces the risk of residue and is often the only detergent permitted. Be sure to check the washing machine before loading for any residue from the last load. Use mesh laundry bags for your favorite clothes, delicates, and small items to protect them during the rough cycles and to prevent them from being accidentally overlooked when you're emptying the machines.

PERSONAL WELLNESS

Challenge: Difficulty Meeting People/Feeling Isolated

Transitioning from a K–12 environment, where you know most of the same people for all those years, to a brand-new campus, away from home, possibly with no familiar faces, is a challenge for most everyone.

Recommended Fix

Keep in mind that you are not alone, and most other freshmen are feeling the same way you are. Some will make friends quickly or may know people from home, but many start out feeling lonely and isolated. It takes time to meet and connect with people, but you get out of it what you put into it. Keep your dorm room door open when you're in your room during the first week. Say yes to invitations, even when you're tired or don't feel an immediate connection with someone. Attend floor meetings and activities, and go to extra help and study sessions even if you don't need help. These early weeks are an ideal time to branch out, as everyone else is also looking to meet new people.

Challenge: No One to Go to the Dining Hall With

It's dinnertime on day 2, your roommate is busy, and you don't want to go to the dining hall by yourself.

Recommended Fix

If it is still daytime, consider asking your classmates if they'd like to meet up for dinner later. If it is later in the day, walk down your hall and look for others who are probably in the same boat. Take a look at the dining hall menu, let others know it is taco or stir-fry night, and ask if they'd like to join you. Even if these options don't pan out, just go. Many students will arrive alone and feeling uneasy. Fill your tray, look for other students dining alone, and ask if they mind if you join them. At the worst, you'll have a quiet and awkward meal with a stranger. Best case, you'll find out you have a lot in common and plan to have dinner together tomorrow night, too.

Challenge: Constantly Not Feeling Well

I often tell families that the first semester of college is like kindergarten all over again: full of sniffles, colds, and sometimes fevers and sore throats. As with kindergarten, you have lots of students in a new environment, in close quarters, and probably nervous and not getting enough sleep.

Recommended Fix

Sleep can cure many things. Prioritize sleep as much as possible. Healthy eating and taking vitamins can also help. If fatigue or illness lingers beyond a week or two, a quick visit to the health center to rule out a bacterial infection is a good idea. Often, the underlying issue beyond germ exposure is poor air quality, possibly including mold hiding in the dorm room, especially in the air vents. Do not accept taking recurring courses of antibiotics without having the dorm room air quality checked or adding a quality air purifier to the room to filter out invisible spores.

HOMESICKNESS

Challenge: Feeling Lonely or Homesick

Even the most social students can be surprised by how much they miss home. Many students call their parents within the first few weeks reporting that they made a poor college choice. This is all normal, and for most, it will subside. Do a Google search for "W-Curve Model for college students" for helpful information.

Recommended Fix

Be empathetic, but don't make changes. As parents of young adults, our job is to listen, let them vent, and empathize, but not to solve their problems. Encourage the student to attend new-student gatherings or a club event, no matter how awkward it feels or whether they have no interest in the topic. Set up specific times for them to call or FaceTime home so the student will know that is on the schedule.

Challenge: Feeling Unprepared or Overwhelmed

Within the first few weeks of starting college, students face higher academic standards or pressures, the search for a friend group, and the adjustment to an entirely new living environment away from the comforts and safety of home.

Recommended Fix

This is all normal! Students will not find their way in a few short weeks and need time to develop new habits, new friendships, and a sense of comfort in this new environment. Controlling what you can control is a great way to feel less overwhelmed. Keep the room neat, do the laundry, and create even small daily habits, such as taking a walk around campus while listening to music or a podcast during an hour-long break between classes. Additionally, locate a reliable hydration station in or near the dorm. Routines help with structure and confidence. Focus on routines, habits, and healthy choices in these early weeks to help you settle in more comfortably.

Challenge: Lack of Downtime

Dorm life can feel like there's a constant buzz and no off switch, which is a lot for those used to refilling their tank with a bit of downtime.

Recommended Fix

Set up a sort of scavenger hunt for yourself. Take an hour or two to walk through campus, seeking out quiet spaces and private areas; there should be many, but they're not well-advertised. Make time to take walks in safe places with headphones and disconnect from the dorm room, the hall, and classes. The rec center may be bustling, but can you watch a show while on a treadmill or riding a stationary bike and block out the surroundings? Come up with four or five outlets and places to escape to when it is time to recharge.

Challenge: Feeling Unsafe or Having a Security Scare

Campuses, whether large or small, rural or urban, can all feel big and even a little scary, especially at night.

Recommended Fix

Always let friends know your plans or share your location via Life360, Find My Friends, or Snap Map. Store campus security's number in your phone as a favorite. Do not wear headphones or earbuds when walking alone at night, and consider carrying a personal alarm or other safety device for added confidence. Better yet, do not walk alone in the evenings except in well-populated areas. Campus security should provide safety escorts and safe rides when necessary. Once you're back at the dorm, keep the door of your room locked, even for short trips to the bathroom, and keep valuables secured and out of sight.

TECHNOLOGY

Challenge: Internet or Wi-Fi Problems

Weak connections are common on crowded campus networks, which are further taxed by streaming during student downtime.

Recommended Fix

Check the college IT page for recommendations. Are there separate Wi-Fi networks for school and streaming? Are there live network ports in the dorm rooms that will support a wired Ethernet connection, which would be much faster?

Challenge: Phone/Laptop Batteries Won't Last Through the Day

Not only is this a common complaint, but it is also essential to have a charged phone for safety purposes.

Recommended Fix

Carry a portable charger (fully charged) every day. You'll need a higher-capacity device to charge a laptop (at least 20,000 mAh with a powerful charging port). Identify which classrooms and study spaces have accessible outlets and charging stations, and plan your activities accordingly. Set the phone to low power mode during class and other busy times—minimizing interruptions is a good thing.

FOOD ISSUES

Challenge: The Food Isn't Great

Schools often feed thousands of students daily in their dining halls, so you shouldn't expect five-star dining.

Recommended Fix

It is time to do a little planning and also get creative. Check the weekly schedules and take advantage of the dining hall when meals that you do like are being offered. At other times, try combining pasta from the pasta bar with toppings from the salad bar and a drizzle of sauce from the international station or a sprinkle of hot sauce from the condiments area. Or load up on simple proteins, vegetables, and fruit if the daily specials aren't appealing. Focus on fueling your body over having a culinary experience. Drink plenty of water, and avoid sugary sodas and other highly sweetened beverages.

Challenge: Being Hungry All the Time

Even with an unlimited meal plan, students will be hungry. Activity schedules make it difficult to get to the dining hall before it closes; inclement weather makes walking to the dining hall less appealing; and late-night munchies are real.

Recommended Fix

Brainstorm simple dorm-friendly meals and snacks. Yogurt, cheese sticks, nuts (be sure your roommate does not have an allergy to them), and protein bars keep well and make good snacks. Microwavable frozen meals, oatmeal, soup, and easy-to-cook pasta dishes are potential meal replacements. Good old peanut butter and jelly sandwiches are a smart, budget-friendly option—use whole-grain bread and keep some in the fridge or freezer. Store all unrefrigerated food in airtight containers to keep it fresh and pest-free.

Key Actions to Take

There are many scenarios here, and plenty more out there that new college students experience every day. As with anything, deep breaths, a positive attitude, and a smile go a long way. If you're upset or angry, sleep on it before responding or reacting; the light of day can often shed a different light on a frustrating challenge. Maybe it can even become a strength—think about how you can turn that frustration into something positive!

If the challenges continue, seek advice from your RA, the campus counseling center, an academic advisor, a member of the local clergy, or your parents. Many of these issues are absolutely normal, but having an unbiased third party to talk things through with is undoubtedly helpful.

23

Planning for Move-Out & Next Year

What You'll Take Away

- A list of what to research for move-out planning
- The steps to take in the last few weeks to get prepared for move-out
- A packing plan for move-out based on summer storage plans
- What to consider and when to book summer storage
- What tools and supplies to bring for move-out day
- Why it is never too early to start thinking about housing for next year

Ideally, you're reading this well before move-out day, as some of these steps are best taken in advance.

The good news is that move-out is much easier than move-in—no months of shopping, no worrying about room setups, and hopefully less stress and emotion than that first big drop-off.

Although moving out is simpler, it still helps to have a plan to avoid last-minute chaos and wasteful decisions.

To alleviate stress and ensure that nothing is overlooked, this chapter guides you through what to do early and what to consider for next year.

THINKING AHEAD TO THE NEXT SCHOOL YEAR

Let's start here, as this is short and sweet and should actually happen long before you're thinking about move-out day.

Housing options are often dictated by the school:

- Some schools require on-campus housing for all four years but may offer suite- or apartment-style options for upperclassmen.
- Some schools guarantee housing only for freshmen, making it very difficult to obtain on-campus housing the following year.

For on-campus housing:

- Find out early in your freshman year what the process is for requesting housing for next year. You will likely need to commit in the first semester of your first year to have returning student selections prior to the incoming freshmen.
- You should be able to commit with or without roommate decisions, but be sure you are thinking about your building

preference, dorm style, and potential roommates long before the housing portal opens for requests or assignments.

For off-campus housing:

- The off-campus housing market can be quite competitive, especially for options closer to campus, and leases for those options may need to be signed as early as September or October of the student's first year, nearly a year in advance.
- Many apartment complexes and even some private homes now require each occupant to sign their own lease. Parents can expect to co-sign the lease and have their credit checked as part of the process.
- Unfortunately, most leases will be one calendar year in length (or maybe a couple of weeks shy of a full year but still require twelve monthly payments).
- Students should tour properties in their budget with potential roommates before committing to a lease.

Questions to ask about off-campus housing:

- How long is the lease term?
- Are any utilities included?
- Are there any other fees not included in the rent or utilities, such as for parking?
- What are the average costs for utilities that are not included?
- Is the space furnished or unfurnished?
- If furnished, what is included, and what are the details on furniture sizes?

A FEW MONTHS BEFORE DORM MOVE-OUT: GET THE BASICS IN ORDER

A little preparation goes a long way, especially when you're working to reduce waste *and* get everything to fit into a car or a storage unit at the end of the school year.

Start with Move-Out Research

Moving out may seem straightforward, but just as with moving in, every school has its own policies. The student should check those about the following:

- **Scheduled Move-Out Times:** Are there assigned move-out times, similar to assigned move-in times that you may have had? Do you need to sign up for a move-out time slot?
- **Check-Out Procedures:** Are there published check-out procedures? Turning in the room and mailbox keys?
- **Parking Rules:** Where are helpers permitted to park on move-out day?
- **Room Condition:** What condition does the school expect you to leave the room in? Is vacuuming or mopping involved?
- **Damage Fines:** Is there a list of fines for damages? You could bring some supplies to handle a few simple repairs, which would help minimize fines.
- **Rental Return Policies:** What is the process for returning rented mini fridges, bed lofts, or any other rented property?
- **Move-Out Assistance:** Even if the school provided helpers at move-in, you will likely not have this assistance at move-out, but please confirm.

Look Into Resale and Donation Options

Plan ahead for all items in the dorm room. Decide what is going home, what's going to storage, what can be resold, what didn't survive, and what needs to be discarded. The rest should be donated.

Resale Options

- Is there a service at the school that facilitates the buying and selling of items between students? These may be referred to as move-out markets or by another name.
- Is there a Facebook Marketplace page connected with the school? This won't be an official school page, but more likely a parent-led one. Join the group early, as for-sale posts go up eight to ten weeks before the end of the spring semester.
- If you're moving off-campus next school year, now could be a good time to pick up furniture for an apartment or house. Graduating students often sell most of their bulky belongings.

Donation Options

- Does the school or someone affiliated with it accept donations of gently used dorm items for students who may need a little help getting their rooms outfitted next year? Will they also accept gently used clothes? Determine their policies and timelines for drop-off or pickup.
- Is there a Facebook Buy Nothing group where you can post items you are giving away?
- What organizations outside of the school accept donations? Habitat for Humanity ReStore, Goodwill, and the Salvation Army may be local and may do school pickups.

Please follow all platform safety recommendations and never meet a buyer or seller alone. Choose a populated area, such as a police station, and bring a friend with you.

Book Time-Sensitive Travel and Storage

- Once the final exam schedule is out, book flights and hotels ASAP—hotels fill up quickly, especially in graduation season.
- If the student isn't bringing everything home, consider reserving shared storage with friends to split costs.

Before booking travel, check the dorm closure dates. Do not plan to move the day after finals end without confirming that the dorm will still be open. If you live within driving distance, you probably won't need to deal with these options unless you plan to arrive the night before move-out.

Coordinate with Roommates

Students should check in with their roommate(s) to coordinate move-out plans together, including:

- Who's taking what: Decide how to divvy up shared items, such as rugs and refrigerators.
- Who's moving out when: Try to arrange it so that everyone isn't in the same space at once.
- Cleaning responsibilities: Depending on the move-out schedule, determine who will take out the final trash and handle the final required cleaning.

Students should also touch base with their RA about any special information regarding move-out from this floor or building.

Start to Bring Things Home During Visits

If the student will be visiting home for spring break, Easter, or another occasion, have them consider bringing home winter clothing, shoes, sports equipment, or other items that they won't need for the remainder of the school year.

The same goes if you will be visiting them at school during the spring. While they're home, be sure to send them back to school with moving bags so that they can pack before you arrive.

Now is a good time to consider where the college gear will be stored for the summer. Create a spot in the basement, their closet, or even a corner of their bedroom. Knowing where an item is going before it arrives will be monumental in terms of not having it left homeless in the foyer or dining room for days or weeks.

IN THE FINAL WEEKS: PREP FOR A SMOOTHER DORM MOVE-OUT

Ideally, students will have everything packed and cleaned when parents arrive for move-out day, but let's be realistic: They'll be busy studying for finals, celebrating with friends, and going to those last meetings, concerts, and end-of-year parties.

Here are some tasks they can accomplish during study breaks:

- Start removing trash. By move-out week, hall and building trash will begin to accumulate. If there are things that need to go, get ahead of the trash pile.
- Take pictures (or use pics from move-in day) to list items for sale on the Facebook Marketplace group that you hopefully found a month or so ago.
- Start using up food items in the fridge and freezer, and stop buying more groceries, especially perishables.

- Sell last semester's textbooks back to the bookstore or return rentals to Amazon. The timing will depend on the class completion date, but it's best to have a plan in place.
- Consolidate open bottles of lotion, shampoo, and other personal care products.
- Throw out/recycle any empty containers or those that don't have enough contents to be of good use.
- Place items to be donated or sold out of the way or in a corner together.
- Find the doorstop: You'll need it again for move-out day.

DETERMINE THE MOVE-OUT CREW AND TRANSPORTATION

Depending on how much the student has to move out and if they have their own vehicle, determine how many cars you'll need to bring in order to ferry it all back home. You'll also want to coordinate family schedules to determine who is available to help! Think about your move-in experience and adjust if you think you had too many or too few people.

PREPARE THE APPLIANCES

One to two days before moving, students need to unplug their fridge to ensure that it is completely defrosted for the move. Remind students to have a towel ready near the fridge to absorb any spills or drips of water.

Try not to use other appliances for the last day to allow them time to dry. This includes coffee makers, hot pots, and electric kettles. You don't want them to get put away and forgotten about for the entire summer with water trapped somewhere inside.

Pro Tip: If you're a parent showing up early in the morning, consider bringing a box of coffee and bagels from a local breakfast place to share with the student's hallmates and any other parents who may be around for move-out at the same time.

TOOLS AND SUPPLIES TO BRING/HAVE ON MOVE-OUT DAY

A suggested list of items to bring from home to help with the move-out is below. And just like on move-in day, bring extras to share with less prepared hallmates and their families.

- A cooler stocked with water and snacks. Bring a large cooler if there are items in the fridge that need to come home.
- A few old blankets to put under the fridge in the car, and around the TV, the coffee maker, and any other delicate items. Remember all those things that arrived in boxes? They now need a safe ride home. You can also use bath towels and bedding to pad the smaller items in moving bags.
- Kitchen or larger trash bags. You'll need them, plus they may come in handy for bulky items.
- Stretch wrap or painter's tape to keep drawers and doors closed; the tape can also be used to label bags and other items. Stretch wrap is also helpful to keep the mattress topper rolled up (never fold it). Alternatively, use belts or Velcro straps.
- Vacuum bags and a vacuum or hand pump to shrink down bedding and clothes if there are concerns about fitting everything in the car.
- A permanent marker to label boxes and bags, or to write on the tape to label the moving bags.

- Gallon ziplock plastic bags. These are great for open toiletries and for storing loose items together and keeping them from falling out of or getting lost in other storage. Use the permanent marker to label the bags.
- A small tool kit with a rubber mallet (unless the student has one at school—if so, remind them not to pack it until after move-out is complete).
- A hand truck if you need to move a fridge or other heavy or bulky items, such as nightstands or chests of drawers.
- Cleaning supplies, if the student doesn't already have them in the dorm.
- Wall repair materials, if needed. Please refer to your leasing/dorm contract for the specific details.
- *All* the moving bags! If you have the moving bags with the little plastic window on the side, bring a few index cards to write the contents of each bag on and put in that plastic holder.
- Tie-down straps if you are placing items on the roof of the car or in the back of a truck.

Pro Tip: Bring a hair dryer if there isn't one in the room. Heating up adhesive on walls or other surfaces makes it really easy to roll up and remove!

DORM MOVE-OUT PACKING PLAN

Before you start putting belongings into moving bags, take an inventory of the items in the dorm room and make plans for their future. If you're moving into another dorm room next year, this should be pretty easy. If you're moving into off-campus housing, you'll have more decisions to make!

Be ready to apply one of these three categories to each item as you pack the room, grouping the categories together.

1. **Summer:** These are items you will need to use over the summer. Label these items as either HOME or SUMMER.
2. **Next School Year:** Not needed over the summer, but you'll use these for the next school year. Label these BACK TO COLLEGE.
3. **Do Not Need:** These are items to consider keeping for a younger sibling, donating, or selling. If you will keep items for a hand-me-down, label those items [SIBLING NAME] COLLEGE SUPPLIES.

When making these decisions, be sure to have a trash bag ready for items that won't be needed and are in a condition that doesn't allow for donation.

START PACKING!

Of course, be sure to separate your belongings from your roommate's before you start packing.

Bedding and Laundry

Remove everything from the bed so you can stand on it to reach the decor above and have better access to what is stored below. Put all items that can or should be laundered into the same moving bag(s) or into the laundry hamper.

You can reserve some bedding or towels to wrap any delicate items. Assuming you will not need the bedding over the summer, bring it home to launder. If you're flying and storing the bedding near school, you will probably want to launder it before storing it.

Mattress Topper

Remove the mattress topper and roll it up tightly, then do one of the following:

- Put it in a kitchen-size trash bag or inside two pillowcases and secure it with duct tape or Velcro straps.
- Wrap it with stretch wrap to keep it rolled in a tight roll.

Do not fold a foam topper. Ensure that the topper stays in room-temperature conditions at home or in storage—avoid letting it get too hot or too cold.

Storage Drawers

If the drawers are going home, will you use them again next year? If yes, fill the drawers with items that need to come back next year, too, such as small items in the desk, kitchen items, and other loose ends that you won't need over the summer.

Tape or stretch wrap the drawers closed. If the drawers are going to storage, you can similarly fill them with items you won't need over the summer, but be sure not to store food, coffee pods, or anything that will attract pests. If you will not use the drawers next year, this is a good item to donate or sell.

Closet Contents

Put clean clothes that are going home into moving bags or suitcases. If you aren't flying, you can place hanging clothes in the moving bag by leaving the hangers out of the short end with the zipper.

Put shoes, belts, accessories, and bags in a separate bag. If shoes are really dirty, they can be placed in a trash bag inside the moving bag.

For any items staying in storage near the school for the summer, such as winter coats and boots, place them in a zipped container or in storage drawers. If you're taking the laundry hamper home, you can fill this with dirty bedding and towels and save a moving bag for other items.

Desk Contents

Bring gallon ziplock bags for small loose items like desk and school supplies. Use a permanent marker to label the bags if necessary. Can these bags fit in the storage drawers?

First Aid/Medications

If your kids are like mine, they'll have a good bit of first aid and OTC medication left over at the end of the school year. Pack this in a place where you can easily access it when you return home to try to make use of these items before their expiration dates.

Bathroom Items

Try to pack all the bathroom, makeup, and hair care items in one bag. Wrap up any breakable items, such as nail polish and jars, in padded toiletry bags or towels. This bag is likely a summer bag to take straight to their room at home upon arrival.

Appliances

It is best to keep the fridge upright during travel and in storage. It should be able to stand up in the back of a minivan or an SUV. If you're moving a microwave, wrap the glass turntable inside if it has one. Depending on the other appliances and their fragility, you can wrap them in a blanket or towel and place them in a moving bag, or carefully transport them to the car.

Laptops and Other Devices

Put the laptop, tablet, and all device chargers in the student's backpack for travel home to make sure they stay together.

Kitchen Items

Wrap and place food storage containers, utensils, water bottles, or anything delicate in a moving bag or even a cleaned-out trash can for storage. If this bag is coming home, take it to the kitchen so that the appliances and containers can get a good deep clean when they get home.

Assembled Furniture

As you disassemble furniture, place all the bolts, screws, and connectors for each piece in a baggie and label the baggie with a permanent marker. If you don't need to disassemble drawers, consider stretch wrap around them to keep them closed during transport.

Wall Decor

Remove wall decor and pack as needed to protect it. Remove adhesive hooks following removal directions exactly, and remove any other materials used to hang things on the walls. Use the materials you brought from home to patch any wall damage. Heating adhesive with a hair dryer makes it easier to remove.

Electronics

Pack TVs, lamps, gaming consoles, and monitors carefully and transport gently to the car.

Rug

If you'll be bringing the rug home or keeping it for next year, vacuum it well before rolling it up. You can put duct tape or stretch wrap around the rolled-up rug to keep it together. Secure in at least three places—near each end and around the middle.

What Are You Missing?

Go back and review your dorm packing checklist to help remember other items you brought that haven't been packed yet.

REFLECT AND DOCUMENT

As you conclude your year in the dorm, take a moment to reflect on the memories you've made. Take pictures with your roommate, your hallmates, and your favorite things in the building and the area. I also took a photo of my son next to his room number sign in the hall. Document it all. These college days fly by, but try to stop and soak in all that you accomplished this year, and hold on to those memories as tightly as you can.

Key Actions to Take

- ☐ Confirm the school's move-out and scheduling process.
- ☐ Review the school's check-out procedures and potential fines for damages in advance; bring simple repair supplies only if permitted.
- ☐ Coordinate with roommates on shared items, cleaning tasks, and who will be present for the final RA inspection.
- ☐ Book travel and storage units early—hotel rooms near campus fill fast during graduation week.

ACKNOWLEDGMENTS

This book was written on an expedited timeline while I was already working more than a full-time job managing The Dorm Guide (the company). I must first thank my family for their patience while I spent months glued to my laptop, day and night. Although I was happy in early retirement for a long time, this book and the company have given me an empty-nest purpose that I didn't know I needed.

To my husband, Greg. Thank you more than anyone else for your patience and endless support, for asking the right questions along the way, and for quietly disappearing into the basement when you could see things boiling over. Thank you for the grocery trips, for expanding your cooking skills, and for keeping Murphy (aka Dorm Dog) busy and tired so that I wouldn't feel guilty looking into antsy puppy eyes.

To my boys, Bryce and Brad. Thank you for letting me learn alongside you, for answering the incredibly detailed questions I randomly text you about your dorm experiences, and for *sometimes* agreeing to be part of the social media content. Your support through this process and willingness to have leftovers for dinner when I was on a deadline were so appreciated. I'm so proud of who you're both becoming, and I will desperately miss your college days in a few years. *The Dorm Guide* began with your college journeys, and I hope it helps countless others begin theirs successfully.

To my Dorm Guide partner in crime, next-door neighbor, and BFF, Jessica Brown. What can I even say? You joined me on this journey around the same time you became an empty-nester, and you haven't looked back for one minute. You and I have worked more hours in the past year than most people do in two, but your dedication and impact have been incredible, and I'm so deeply grateful. Thank you for shouldering all of it while I was holed up for weeks at a time writing this book—I could not have gotten it done without your support and understanding.

To friends and family who regularly asked "How's the book going?" I wasn't telling you the half of it. It was an incredibly aggressive timeline and a level of concentration and focus that I did not think I had in me, so I thank you for checking in and understanding the short replies and declined invitations, and I look forward to catching up with all of you now that this book is done!

My deepest thanks to my editor, Molly Birnbaum, and her editorial assistant, Laine Whittier. Your amazingly patient guidance, thoughtful suggestions, and constant smiling optimism carried me through this, and I can't thank you enough. Your belief in this project and willingness to move it through the process quickly boosted my focus and brought momentum to every chapter. My gratitude extends to the entire team at Ten Speed Press and Penguin Random House—Lizzie Allen, Liana Faughnan, Andrea Lau, and Dan Myers.

To the many families and followers with me along the way,

thank you. I've heard your desperation looking for just the right dorm essentials for your kids, felt your combined excitement and dread as move-in day nears, and understood your sadness yet sense of accomplishment on the way home. I feel like I know you, even though we've not met in person. This book would not exist without this extraordinary community of parents and students who have shared their questions, challenges, and insights with me over the years. Your generosity, humor, and willingness to learn from one another shaped this guide in so many ways, and I thank you for trusting me to walk alongside you during this emotional milestone era in our lives.

To the reader, thank you for trusting me and picking up *The Dorm Room Guide*. Even though I've studied everything in this book for years, tested products, collected all of the feedback, dreamed up creative solutions, and made a huge mess with the dorm room in my house overflowing into just about every other part of it, I'm still learning every day. And I will continue learning. I hope you'll join me on socials and on the website to be a part of all of the latest learnings, tips, and ideas, and to share your questions and feedback, too.

RESOURCES

The Dorm Room Guide was born out of years of research, writing, and testing for TheDormGuide.com and social media channels. While the suggestions in this book are timeless, new products and solutions continue to evolve. Please follow along to get the latest information and product recommendations and to stay organized and confident throughout your college journey.

You can find all referenced materials from this book at TheDormGuide.com/bookresources.

INDEX

S

T

U

V

W

Y

ABOUT THE AUTHOR

LARA BECKER is the founder of The Dorm Guide, a nationally trusted, all-encompassing online platform that helps families prepare for college and dorm life. Recognizing an unsustainable pattern of fads and conjecture in dorm shopping, Lara provides practical, timeless guidance, detailed how-tos, and affordable solutions to optimize the college dorm room experience, from planning and setting up to moving out. Celebrated for her thoughtful, research-based advice, Lara has been featured in *The New York Times* and *The Wall Street Journal.*

TEN SPEED PRESS
An imprint of the Crown Publishing Group
A division of Penguin Random House LLC
1745 Broadway
New York, NY 10019
tenspeed.com
penguinrandomhouse.com

A Ten Speed Press Trade Paperback Original

Library of Congress Control Number: 2026931694

ISBN 9798217036530
Ebook ISBN 9798217036547

Editor: Molly Birnbaum | Production editor: Liana Faughnan
Editorial assistant: Laine Whittier
Cover designer: Derek Thornton / Notch Design | Text designer: Andrea Lau
Production: Dan Myers
Copy editor: Sibylle Kazeroid | Proofreaders: Robin Slutzky, Miriam Taveras, Sigi Nacson, Andrea Peabbles, and Chris Fortunato | Indexer: J S Editorial, LLC
Publicist: Natalie Yera-Campbell | Marketer: Stephanie Davis

Manufactured in the United States of America

1st Printing

First Paperback Edition

The authorized representative in the EU for product safety and compliance is Penguin Random House Ireland, Morrison Chambers, 32 Nassau Street, Dublin D02 YH68, Ireland, https://eu-contact.penguin.ie.